VISUAL TOOLS

FOR DIFFERENTIATING READING & WRITING INSTRUCTION

Roger Essley

with Linda Rief & Amy Levy Rocci

SCHOLASTIC

NEW YORK • TORONTO • LONDON • AUCKLAND • SYDNEY
MEXICO CITY • NEW DELHI • HONG KONG • BUENOS AIRES

Acknowledgments

This book grew from small experiments with visual tools in our classrooms. We want to thank our students for showing us, through their struggles and breakthroughs, that we needed to do more in order to nurture and sustain their learning. The students convinced us that our collaboration was essential to develop and integrate what they were showing us.

What started as a three-way collaboration became the work of many classrooms. We need to thank teachers and their students in many states, and at all grade levels, for experimenting with these evolving tools and then sharing their practical results with us. The sleek tellingboards you see here, designed to fit in any writing folder, were the invention of teachers in a small town in New Hampshire, who found the clunky, oversized storyboards a hassle. Ideas about storyboards for reading comprehension came from teachers in upstate New York and reading specialists in southern Virginia. Early on we had essential encouragement from long-time researchers like Donald Graves and Tom Newkirk to widen the literacy circle. Thank you also to Ruth Culham, for reading our words and seeing our thinking so thoughtfully.

We are especially grateful to the editorial, design, production, and marketing professionals at Scholastic—Terry Cooper, Joanna Davis-Swing, Virginia Dooley, Gloria Pipkin, Sarah Longhi, Jaime Lucero, Susan Kolwicz, and Kelli Thompson—who have given their time, ideas, support, encouragement, expertise, and perspectives to bringing Visual Tools to life and into more teachers' classrooms. Thank you.

Copyedited by David Klein
Edited by Gloria Pipkin
Production editing by Sarah Longhi

Cover design by Brian LaRossa
Interior design by Kelli Thompson
Interior illustrations by Roger Essley

ISBN-13 978-0-439-89908-6
ISBN-10 0-439-89908-7

Contents

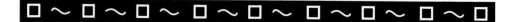

Foreword

Reading this book, I was struck by the simple notion that, as teachers, we can make learning really hard. Certainly we don't mean to, but by narrowing the experiences students have to those that are text-related, rather than creating a rich palette of learning opportunities that engage all students, we make school an impossible place for learners with different styles to succeed. School-learning becomes an isolated activity made up of reading text, interpreting text, creating text. Although this activity may be fine for strong readers and writers—in other words, the traditionally "good student"—it's not okay for others. What about the special education student who's hungry to read but says she can't make pictures in her mind as she goes? What about the second-language student who does not hear English in his head or see the images clearly as he writes? Or what about the wonderfully average student who is simply swamped by the amount of text she must consume in an average day?

It's not okay for us to limit these students by expecting them to learn and show evidence of that learning only through standard text-based reading and writing. And contrary to current practice, it doesn't serve the high-achieving students well either. Their text-bound world of learning is far too narrow to prepare them for the broad spectrum of tasks they will undertake once they leave school, even if they are the traditional, successful achievers.

By relying on text as the primary tool for learning, we ignore the true way many of our students gather and process information. Over the years, we've honed our teaching skills and learned how to differentiate instruction for students needing more time, simpler text, and collaboration. But as Essley, Rief, and Rocci state so clearly in this practical, user-friendly book, there is far more to differentiation than that. Drawing, talking, using storyboards, and thinking aloud, for example, provide students with alternative ways to express what they think and what they know.

The authors show, through many examples and case studies, how learning becomes easier for students when they are taught how to storyboard, or lay out the details of what they want to say in pictures on index cards taped to a storyboard template so they can add, delete, and move them around. Learning to use storyboards, the authors tell us, helps students "stalled by text" to understand what they read and create original works.

I was struck by Linda Rief's account of students who had floundered until Essley visited the classroom and provided strategies for drawing as thinking. These were students who had been nurtured, supported, and honored and who had the benefit of the best practices in language arts. Yet there were still some students who struggled until they learned to storyboard and draw to show what they knew.

I wanted to stand up and cheer when I read about Amy Rocci's third-grade class, where students transition from learning how to read to reading comfortably in order to learn, and how she used storyboarding successfully with struggling readers and writers.

But most of all, I became a believer when I read Essley's compassionate exploration of the problems his own son, Andy, faced as he tried to master learning in a text-centered classroom. Essley taught Andy how to storyboard and make pictures in his mind and on paper, and the achievements of both father and son are inspiring. The strategies that helped Andy succeed and thrive should be embraced by all teachers, for every teacher has students like Andy, who deserve every opportunity to learn and should receive the accolades so often reserved for the more traditional student.

From this book, I take away important thinking. We have to widen the path to learning for students—all students—by adding new techniques to our repertoire. We must arm ourselves with the tools used so effectively in the talented and gifted classrooms: varied teaching and learning strategies designed to engage and inspire the learner. To differentiate reading instruction truly means so much more than putting a different book in the hand of a struggling reader. To differentiate writing instruction truly means so much more than handing students a graphic organizer to show them how to structure their five-paragraph essays. The learning choices we offer students must tap into more than reading and writing continuous text as the sole means of gathering and providing ideas and information. We must teach students how to think. By encouraging students to draw what they think and talk about how their ideas are developing, we give them tools that will serve them well throughout school and life. As Essley reminds us, there is "a big cohort of us out there—school survivors—who discover how easily we can learn after we leave school."

As you enter the world of storyboarding, you will find strategies that you can use right away. In this text are suggestions for how to introduce the technique to your students, step-by-step plans to support you along the way, and examples from real classrooms of what the technique looks like in action. You can dive into storyboarding equipped with all the tools you need. And not to worry: If you don't consider yourself an artist, stick figures will do just fine. Thank goodness!

You are in for a refreshing approach to teaching and learning as you read *Visual Tools for Differentiating Reading and Writing Instruction*. I hope the ideas inspire you to try storyboarding to help all students gain their rightful place in the literacy circle.

Ruth Culham
Author of *6+1 Traits of Writing*

Introduction

Why Use Storyboards?

If I can't picture it I can't understand it.
—Einstein

It is impossible even to think without a mental picture.
—Aristotle

For the boys in our study, the intense importance of the visual as they engaged with all forms of texts was evident, and we believe it cannot be oversold. The few engaged readers in this study all described their reading of books and stories in strikingly visual terms. The other boys described their engagement with visual or multimedia texts, such as movies and cartoons, in much the same enthusiastic way as the engaged readers described their reading. . . . All of the boys insisted that the best materials were highly visual or stimulated visual thinking. Engaged readers like Neil said to read well, it had to be a visual experience. It was important to "see" what he was reading.
—Smith & Wilhelm (2002, pp. 151–152)

A book for teachers focused on drawing and telling as writing tools may seem a tad strange, especially in a time when mandated literacy testing leaves little room for extras or frills. Yet students struggling with literacy need these tools urgently.

Woven throughout this practical book are stories from many classrooms where struggling students of all ages successfully use targeted visual/verbal tools as a bridge to text. We'll see how storyboards with simple drawing increase weak readers' comprehension skills and engage older, reluctant writers for the first time.

Reaching struggling students is important, but I hope you'll see the larger message their work sends. Teachers find these simple tools make learning easier for all students. In fact, the same visual tools that engage the reluctant writer have long been used as the secret weapon of teachers in the gifted and talented class to make instruction more engaging for those different learners who need more challenges.

PRACTICAL DIFFERENTIATED INSTRUCTION

"Different" learning is the key here. If we want to reach all our learners, we need tools that work for them. Offering learning choices is the essential goal of differentiated instruction, but addressing students' different learning styles can be tough to accomplish in a jam-packed curriculum that assumes all kids must read to learn, and write to show what they know. How can we engage and support learners who have trouble reading and writing at grade level, especially when text is our central teaching tool, and achieving proficiency with text is our primary goal?

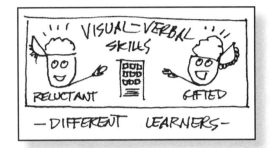

Here's the good news: Teachers who initially try alternative tools as a means of reaching their text-challenged learners often discover they can tap powerful learning potential that just can't be reached with text alone. In fact, teachers find they can reach learners with a broad range of skills—using the same tools. Let me give an example that is close to home.

Andy's Story-Building Tools

When my son Andy began working on his first fiction assignment in his middle school Language Arts class, I knew we were in for trouble. It took a couple of weeks before I got a call from his teacher, who told me she was stuck. Her usual writing techniques, and some serious one-on-one instruction, had barely gotten Andy started. She was confronting learning issues Andy's Individual Educational Plan (IEP) only hinted at. Andy is a concrete thinker. He can play a mean game of chess, brainstorm several moves in advance, and respond to changing events, but ask him to brainstorm a simple made-up story in text and he flounders.

I know kids stalled by text can be a challenge to any teacher, even the great ones. As a text-challenged student myself, I was sent to the psychologist in third grade, because reading and writing were so difficult for me. Eventually, I learned that writing was something other kids did. It took 30 years to unlearn that deeply held lesson. I desperately wanted my son to have a different school experience. I tried suggesting at IEP meetings that low-text alternative tools worked better for Andy, but his teacher assured us Andy would respond to her well-honed (text-focused) writing lessons. Now she was stuck, and I heard the unspoken question implicit in the call: "If a student can't brainstorm a simple story, then what can I do?"

Andy's Board

When Andy's teacher and I agreed that traditional techniques were not working for him, I suggested Andy try some serious storyboarding at home over winter vacation. I got Andy some poster board and file cards and told him he needed to storyboard the story he was working on. After some initial protests that he didn't need Dad's help, he got to work. Andy discussed his story ideas and put them down on the cards, using stick pictures and a few key words. As he taped them to the board, the cards became the building blocks of his story. The pictures made his ideas concrete and visible. They helped him invent a believable character and get a plot going. Now he could see how his story might grow.

During his vacation, Andy brought his almost-finished story—about a boy lost in the White Mountains—with him to his mother's office at the nearby university. He was a little embarrassed by it. He liked his story, but a board covered with stick pictures was not his idea of a cool thing to take to a university. He'd almost made it to his mom's office when a grad student he'd met saw his board and asked, "What's that?" Andy mumbled something about writing a story for school when the grad student interrupted. "That's a storyboard. I'm learning to use those, too!" He explained that his storyboards were part of a graduate business course. "Several of us are designing a business plan to present to NASA. We're using storyboards to brainstorm, write, and prepare our presentation. It's a national competition." The tentative middle school writer and the accomplished grad student discussing pictures as a sophisticated writing tool—Andy became a bit less reluctant.

STORYBOARDS IN MANY PROFESSIONS

Andy was only vaguely aware of the way storyboards helped him organize his ideas and write. The grad student, long accomplished in text, was learning why storyboards are the tool of choice for many professions for brainstorming, collaborative writing, strategic planning, oral presentations, and more.

Storyboards are time-tested writing/thinking tools; they have long been used by writers, scientists, engineers, filmmakers, and many other professionals. It is no coincidence that the same visual tool that helped Andy get started writing is used by the MBA professor to prepare his grad students for the competitive digital world. It's important to note that text-accomplished folks in the real world choose targeted visual tools because they work better than text alone for many thinking and communication tasks.

By the way, that graduate student's team won a national first prize with its storyboard presentation to NASA, and my son wrote a solid text story that he actually liked (a big prize for him).

Andy and the grad student were certainly different learners, but these effective visual tools furthered both their learning goals. Grasping the power of visual tools to connect learners is great news for the classroom. We'll see how targeted visual tools make differentiation natural and easy because low-text tools take learners where they want to go, in third grade, in middle school, and beyond, into their digital/visual future.

CLASSROOM-TESTED TOOLS

Exploring the power of visual tools, especially simple drawings, may be new territory for many teachers, but the tools presented here have been designed and refined in real classrooms like yours. These tools are not hard to use, and they don't require expensive equipment or *any artistic skill*. You'll learn how storyboards fit easily in any classroom and how teachers at all grade levels can use visual/verbal tools to make their classrooms more inclusive and their curriculum more engaging. You'll see in practical detail how offering students a choice of paths to the same goal makes differentiated instruction a daily reality.

Bad Drawing Is Fine—Really!

This book will provide the practical how-to, the nitty-gritty stuff you need to get started storyboarding, and students' work, to show why you should take precious time to try these tools in your classroom. Don't worry if you draw badly—that can actually be a strength: Your students will enjoy teaching you how to use simple stick pictures as a thinking/writing tool. You'll find that students of all ages enjoy the lighthearted drama of stick pictures, and they quickly learn how powerful simple pictures are as a way of conveying their ideas: brainstorming a story, preparing for a test, revising an essay, making notes from a textbook, or practicing an oral presentation.

Indeed, students often intuitively grasp the added value of using pictures as a thinking tool. When we offer real alternatives to text, students often choose storyboards for the same reason adults choose them—they work.

Not Just for Special Education

Special educators may recognize variations of these visual/verbal tools. They are sometimes used in Special Education to address serious learning problems. But beware: if we think of these tools simply as "visual aids" or "accommodations" for struggling students, we are missing their essential power for all learners.

Our current curricula are text-focused because we know all students will need text literacy to participate in our complex world. We can easily expand our practice with visual tools that pull more students into the literacy circle. Making reading and writing more engaging is enough reason to start using these tools, but there are other reasons. When we offer students visual tools

integrated with their text skills, we're also helping them compete in a digital age where text and images are intimately linked. From Web design to new brain-imaging techniques, the literate student today needs to be able to communicate ideas in text and images.

Not Just for Kids

Teachers tell me that once they start using visual tools with their students, those tools become part of their own teaching style. Teachers who initially said, *I'm not visual, I can't draw a straight line*, find themselves easily using drawing as an everyday teaching tool. As they watch visual tools boost students' learning, they find their own natural visual skills support and focus their teaching. That's differentiation at its best. As Carol Ann Tomlinson, a central architect of differentiated instruction says, "The way to get there is to teach [teachers] to look at kids as individuals and to let kids show you what they can do." (Hess, 1999, "Teachers Can Benefit")

WHAT ARE STORYBOARDS?

Before we go into the classroom and see storyboards at work, I want to give a quick overview of what storyboards are and how we've adapted them to best serve learners in the classroom.

Storyboarding, or picture writing, is the origin of all written languages, used by ancient cultures before text evolved and as a natural bridge to text. The Chinese language was built using pictographs. Egyptians used storyboards, or hieroglyphics, first etched in stone and later written on papyrus, to organize a complex society and to rule the ancient world.

Look at any comic strip and you'll see picture writing in action. A storyboard is a writing format, generally a set of boxes (or rectangles, circles, or other shapes) placed in a logically sequenced order. Each box or frame is a place for the writer to put information, pictures, symbols, or text.

Storyboards appear in many forms, from emerging literacy books to emergency instructions on airplanes to technical textbooks. When writers in

various fields want to make ideas easily understood, they choose a storyboard format or one of its close cousins: the flow chart, the time line, or the Power-Point presentation. Storyboards are widely used because we know pictures combined with text offer a rich synthesis of information that can entertain and inform. The pictures in picture writing can be simple cartoons, photographs, or sophisticated technical diagrams.

Stick Pictures and Text

The low-tech storyboards I use in the classroom are designed to show students a clear path to text. We use simple stick pictures combined with spare text as our essential writing style. Offering students hands-on drawing has many advantages over using premade images or clip art. A central benefit of stick pictures is that kids can do it themselves, and they like to draw. As we explore drawing as a differentiation tool, it is important to recognize that the act of drawing, like the act of writing text, is satisfying and informative. Putting pencil to paper, making symbols in pictures or text, helps our ideas to grow.

It is the logical sequencing power of storyboards, combined with the hands-on engagement of drawing, that makes these tools work for learners.

Teachers long comfortable with teaching almost exclusively with text often ask, "What if a student is reluctant to draw?" I've never had a student, from first to twelfth grade, who couldn't use stick pictures in some form. Once students and teachers start using drawing as a thinking tool, it becomes second nature. You'll see students develop their own style, quickly adapting a mix of text and simple stick pictures to fit their skills and needs, whether they're in third grade or eighth grade.

Here is a basic six-square storyboard format from teacher Amy Rocci's third-grade classroom.

The purpose of this storyboard was to see if students could retell the main events of a fairy tale. All the basics of storyboarding in the classroom are evident in this student's work. Students were asked to retell the fairy tale using sequenced boxes containing both stick pictures and spare text—a few key words—in each square. Through her storyboard, this student conveys what she thinks are the six main events in the story. In a sense, she is creating the visual equivalent of a bulleted outline of main points. Note how her pictures and the text support and reinforce each other; together they tell the whole story.

A storyboard can be any length—two or two thousand squares. A storyboard can be simple like the Cinderella board, or elaborate and dense in content like a graphic novel.

Storyboards also can be adapted to fit many tasks, from maps to time lines. Like making text lists down a page or writing text across the page, the way we arrange storyboard boxes can help convey the logic of the task at hand, and make that task easier to accomplish. To convey content, organization boxes can be arranged vertically or horizontally, or set in meaningful clusters.

FORMAT VARIATIONS

See Appendix B, pages 134–140 for descriptions and reproducible pages of several different story-board formats.

Path to Text

It is important to note that whenever text-writing is the goal, the storyboard format offered to students should create a clear path to text. Generally I empha-size formats that parallel writing syntax; squares are written and read across the page the same way we read lines of text, starting in the top left square, returning at the end of each line.

The other main format that creates a clear path to text is boxes with text lines beside them. I generally use this format after a story or essay has been brainstormed and revised. This format allows students to see the direct link between their story-board and sentences or paragraphs of text.

The Tellingboard: Brainstorming and Revision Made Easy

Earlier I described Andy using a board with cards to build and revise his story. He was using what I call a tellingboard, a larger-scale storyboard with movable cards, designed to allow easy brainstorming and revision. This tool makes building a story, an essay, or an oral presentation easier because the writer has hands-on, cut-and-paste capability like a word processor. As we go forward we'll see this tool can be used for many tasks, from writing to reading to revision and conferencing—making them more engaging and effective.

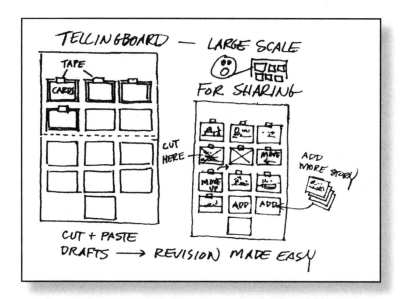

The tellingboard is a large-scale storyboard designed with moveable cards to allow easy drafting and revision of ideas. I recommend an 11-by-17-inch board that folds to fit in any writing folder. To learn how to make a telling-board, see pages 97–99.

Simple Is Best

The Cinderella example on page 11 might look like baby stuff. Don't be fooled. A storyboard is supposed to look simple, to make information visible and clear. The student's job was to summarize the main events in order, and she did a fine job. Her storyboard can be easily "read" and understood by anyone who knows the Cinderella story. You'll see the same simplicity in older students' storyboards, but a closer look will show that their simple pictures efficiently encapsulate sophisticated ideas, as seen in the excerpt from a character analysis storyboard of *Macbeth* at right.

Macbeth's potent vision, highlighted in a student's notes about his character

The use of simple tools is the real strength of storyboarding in the classroom; the same writing process can be used by kindergarteners and graduate engineers or law students. In fact, the law student's notes integrating text and pictures are easier to read and more potent because the stick-pics provide landmarks in pages of dense text. I find students often learn to storyboard faster than adults. I encourage older students to try and storyboard as simply and clearly as a sharp third grader. Whether you are retelling a fairy tale or developing a complex plot for a novel, simple often turns out to be better.

Chapter 1

Storyboarding as a Bridge to Text

Y ou saved my son's life." This phone message got my full attention. I'd never met the woman or her son, but as she told me his story, it sounded all too familiar. "Aaron was doing fine in school until this year, third grade," she said. "I could tell something was wrong before his teacher called me in to tell me he was not writing. She had tried to help, but now she didn't know what to do. I could tell she was worried about Aaron, and I was, too. Aaron used to like school. Suddenly he had started saying, 'Do I have to go?' every morning."

That question, "Do I have to go?" brought back a flood of memories. I know how that story goes; I'm something of an expert on school failure myself. It turned out that Cris, Aaron's mom, had heard me speak at a PTA convention. I'd begun my presentation on visual tools for writers by talking about my own experience as a "learning disabled" student. In the third grade I was sent to the psychologist because I was having a hard time with reading and writing. The psychologist's tests confirmed what the teachers already knew: learning problems. But what could they do?

"As I heard you talk about struggling with text," Cris said, "I thought, 'Aaron is just like you.'"

My mom thought I was smart, too—at home. In school, everybody could see I was slow. Mom got flash cards and worried. Dad's worry became frustra-

tion that I was lazy; he sent me to my room to plow through endless homework. I hoped Aaron hadn't learned yet what I'd learned—if good teachers couldn't help me I must be really dumb. Eventually, I read slowly, wrote painfully, and spent a lot of time drawing World War II B-17 bombers that I imagined were so well defended they couldn't be shot down. But the pop quizzes kept coming, and my teachers said, "Stop drawing and get to work!" I prayed for blizzards and became an expert at cooking up low fevers with a glass thermometer held up to a bed lamp.

At the PTA convention I talked about school failure and how I only learned I could write long after I left school. I demonstrated the way

authors use storyboards to write books. Then I showed how I'd adapted storyboards for the classroom, working with teachers who were trying to help their reluctant writers.

Helping Students With Learning Problems

Cris said, "On the way home from hearing you speak, I thought about Aaron's struggles and what you'd said about visual tools. So I stopped at Staples and bought the materials you'd suggested. I explained to Aaron what you showed us; he got it right away. Now, suddenly, he's writing like crazy. His teacher called to tell me he was suddenly writing in class. She asked, 'What happened? What did you do?'"

Cris gave her son a poster board with file cards taped on it. She made him a storyboard (a simple tellingboard, really) and showed him how he could tell his story with the cards, using simple stick pictures and a few key words.

The storyboard let Aaron get his story down on paper; it was like making a simple comic with stick pictures and text. He made a loose visual outline, working comfortably without the difficulty of using exacting text. Once he could see his full story on paper, he could grow and revise the story by adding or moving cards until his story felt right. Once Aaron was sure what he wanted to tell, and he practiced telling the story from his storyboard, *then* he was ready to write it down. This caring mom showed her son how easily he could use comfortable skills he brings to school every day, drawing and telling, as a bridge to a new and difficult skill, writing text.

A few months later, Cris called again. "You won't believe it!" she said. "Aaron storyboarded a whole book. He just won a citywide writing prize for his first picture book—a story about ants." She was thrilled that her son now enjoyed the process of writing and no longer looked for reasons not to go to school.

Aaron's breakthrough is another confirmation of a clear pattern many teachers have witnessed—from third graders who "can't" write to eighth graders who won't write. When these students work with storyboards in the classroom, something finally clicks, and they jump into writing.

Students like Aaron have shown their teachers that they will write if they can develop their ideas in a low-text format, using drawing and telling to grow ideas before committing them to text. If you've never seen how eagerly kids stalled by text embrace storyboards, it can be hard to believe that a simple choice of tools can make such a difference.

While variations of storyboards are used in many fields, from book publishing to engineering, in adapting storyboards for the classroom I've focused on creating formats designed to create a clear path to text writing. Aaron saw intuitively how his storyboard created a logical step-by-step writing process that would let him build a story and then transform it into text.

HELPING STUDENTS WITH READING COMPREHENSION

Storyboards are not just for writing. While I started working with storyboards as a writing tool, it became evident that the technique could be adapted for many literacy tasks. Perhaps most important was discovering the way storyboards work to support reading comprehension. This should not be surprising. Research shows the key to comprehension is visualization—making mental pictures (Bell, 1991). We will explore why storyboards are a natural visualization tool, uniquely suited to helping learners in the classroom make fleeting mental pictures concrete and memorable.

STUDYING FAILURE: SHARING THE GOOD NEWS

As I said earlier, I'm something of an expert on failure. Like Aaron, I was stalled by text early on, but I stayed stalled. Long after school, I thought of myself as a "disabled" learner and a confirmed reluctant writer. I know how Aaron felt when he suddenly discovered that he could write, but my own writing break-through came at the age of 40. I wrote a picture book. It was published, and I suddenly found myself speaking in schools as the "visiting author."

As I visited many classrooms, I wanted to learn why I'd been so slow to write and what I could do to help kids in a similar position. It may be hard for those who did well in school to imagine what school is like for the other half. I've said I was slow at reading and writing. I often reversed letters and numbers, so math was a nightmare, too. Eventually I did learn to read. I wrote, too, but only if I was forced. In a world that measures academic achievement through reading and writing skills—the college essay and the SAT—I was at a severe disadvantage.

After high school I followed a careful reluctant writer's career plan. I went to art school, where reading and writing were not the primary skills valued by professors. The focus was visual thinking and showing what you know visually: by designing a car, creating a film, or building a story in pictures.

I did pretty well working as an artist. Some of my drawings, visual stories built with layers of family snapshots, are owned by museums. Looking at those drawings now, it's not hard to see how telling family stories in pictures might lead to writing.

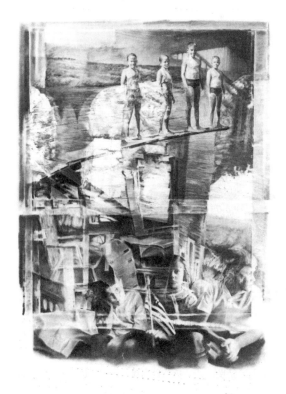

This is one of my large black-and-white drawings. In these pictures, I combine three generations of family snapshots—my own, my father's, and my grandparents'—fusing images from different eras into a mosaic about relationships, hopes, and dreams.

My hope that I could avoid writing as an artist was clearly naive. I found this out for sure when a curator at the Metropolitan Museum of Art in New York called to tell me I needed to write "a standard artist's statement for the museum's archives" about two of my drawings the museum owned. Another person might have considered writing an artist's statement an exciting opportunity. I panicked. Making pictures, I looked smart, but I'd learned in school that I always look stupid when I write. And archives meant people could read my lame artist's statement even after I was dead and see that I was dumb. In the end, my wife "helped" me write that statement.

Then one day I was sitting alone in my studio, drawing from an old family snapshot, when I got a story idea: a boy climbs into an old family photo; he meets his great-grandfather (as a boy), and they have adventures in the past. I remembered my grandparents' stories about life long ago. In my head I could see the whole story, all the images of horses and Model Ts on the farm. I thought, "This could be a picture book. I'd draw the pictures, and I'd tell a writer friend my story, *and he could write it.*" But something inside told me that I no longer needed to have someone else do my writing. That day, I sat at the computer. I began typing with one finger.

This is a picture from my book *Reunion* (1994), a time-travel story about a boy who climbs into an old family photo.

A Reluctant Writer Heads Back to School

That first story was eventually published (after nearly 100 drafts). At one of my book signings, an enthusiastic teacher persuaded me to speak at her school. I arrived nervous, armed with lots to show: sketches, finished artwork, manuscripts, dummy books, research materials. I was introduced to a gym full of kids: "We are so pleased to have a successful writer with us today. . . ."

The kids beamed at me. But I couldn't start. The shock of being called a successful writer was too much. Soon I was confessing I wasn't a *real writer* at all. I found myself telling those kids about my school failures and about the excitement of learning I could write, but only long after I'd escaped school. To my astonishment, the teachers said it was an inspirational presentation, and more invitations followed.

Masquerading as the "visiting author" was an eye-opener. Telling kids about learning to write was fun, but audiences always wanted me to talk more about failure. After my presentations, kids would wait off to the side to confide, "This was the best assembly. I'm slow like you." Teachers would linger, help me pack up, and say quietly, "Our students need to hear more from adults about struggling in school. But my colleagues need to hear you, too. I have a smart child being left behind. They have no idea. . . ."

Struggling Students Helping Each Other

Public talks led to private meetings with teachers who began asking, "Could you meet with Sally? She is struggling." I found myself talking with a shy girl in a corner of the library, or sitting across from a big, sulky boy in the Special Ed room. At first I was nervous meeting with "slow" kids like me, wondering what I could offer, but I quickly learned we had a lot in common. I saw how frustrated these kids were in school, and how eager they were to connect, to share what they could do beyond reading and writing. Kids told me stories, showed me pictures, and shared ideas about music and TV and mousing around in the digital world.

Still, when kids talked about school, it was depressing. Invited to motivate a group of struggling students, I asked how they felt about writing. They said flatly they were all "bad" at it. I asked how they knew. One said, as if I were a dummy, "We all did bad on the state test." A girl offered her official writing sample as evidence. She warned me, "It's bad. I got a 2." Her story was fine, but she'd made a fundamental mistake: She'd veered from the narrow writing prompt and written about something she cared about. The state test made reluctant writing a certainty.

An eighth-grade girl, withdrawn and wary, showed me her required Language Arts journal. It was all but empty. When I asked what she liked to do, I got the sad "nothing" reply. She'd been told I was a writer, but when I mentioned I liked to draw, she got up, went to her backpack, and offered up a ratty notebook.

It was a visual diary, full of smudged cartoon drawings, titles here and there, short captions. Studying a drawing of a girl with a don't-mess-with-me look, I asked, "What's this story?" The girl eyed me, surprised I knew there was a story in every picture. She smiled and launched into, "Okay, this girl is having a bad hair day. . . . People don't like her, see, her books got knocked on the floor, they think she's dumb, but she . . ."

After several stories poured out, I asked if she'd ever drawn a picture in her Language Arts journal. She looked at me like I was nuts. I understood. I'd seen the other all-print journals. Pictures were not what the Language Arts teacher was looking for.

GETTING PAST THE LABELS

When I talked with these kids' teachers, they readily acknowledged the paradox I saw: these were mostly bright kids who were stalled in school. The teachers were frank; they simply didn't know what to do.

Increasingly, I drove home from school visits acutely aware of how different my life had been since I escaped from school. It had taken a long time, but in the real world, I'd learned I wasn't stupid or slow. Now that I was writing, many new doors were open to me. I was frustrated it had taken me so long to start. And I wanted to know where my learning problems had suddenly gone.

About that time I chanced on two magazine articles about well-known authors. They were worlds apart—one a big-time TV writer, the other a serious novelist—but both told school failure stories that were strikingly familiar. Both talked about how surprising it was to find that they could write and that they were not stupid or slow, except in school. Those articles

prompted me to start asking other adults about their school experiences. It turns out there is a big cohort of us out there—school survivors—who discover how easily we can learn after we leave school.

UNDERSTANDING THE TEXT BIND

As soon as I considered the possibility that many learning problems could be a by-product of how we teach, identifying the most common source of school failure seemed easy: *Text was too hard for many students.*

School is built on an expanding pyramid of skills. We start with "the basics"—reading and writing—and we progress to diverse content introduced and reinforced with text. From a child's point of view, this weighty learning pyramid rests on one narrow point—text, and that means if you are text-smart, you will look smart in school and be rewarded daily. But, if you are text-slow, everybody in school will know you are slow at everything that really counts—and you'd just better grit your teeth and try to survive.

Looking at school from this back-row point of view may seem negative. To suggest our practice leaves kids behind can seem critical of teachers, but please stay with me; there is a silver lining. Paradoxically, considering that students' learning may be stalled by *text itself* can offer us an exciting window onto a new learning landscape. If a lot of school failure is caused by text itself, that might mean an alternative path to text could enable us to address much of this failure at its source.

It can be hard for those comfortable with text to see how text might create a serious education problem—and that's the rub. From kindergarten on, all of us were steeped in the idea that text is central to good learning. By the time they took away the blocks and crayons, it was clear all the "smart" kids were learning to read and write well. These early lessons go deep, and by the time we leave school, we've all seen text competence connected with successful learning for so long that we unconsciously view them as the same thing. To get respectable scores on the SATs, you must have good text skills, and those who do well are rewarded with entrance to the best colleges and the best jobs.

To seriously consider the proposition that many competent learners are stalled by text in school, we need to crack that good learner = good-at-text nut. From the back row, it's not hard to see that reading and writing text are what we teach and how we deliver content, and that text skills are how we measure achievement. That means competence with text skills becomes the narrow gateway to all learning, from introducing content to class discussion to showing what you know on the test or the essay.

In classrooms with older students, where content is often introduced and reinforced through independent reading, poor comprehension clearly hamstrings both learners and teachers. The limiting effects of text are directly acknowledged in tracking, where lowered expectations become the norm for kids with poor text skills. Parents are often told, "Your child will be more comfortable in the lower track because the regular classes do a lot more reading and writing."

An outside observer might ask, "Why do you lower learning expectations for those students—why not address their poor comprehension issues head-on?" If we try to answer that question, we bang directly into text as a learning problem. The uncomfortable truth is that educators know reading problems (and associated poor writing skills) are tough to address. We know because we've tried again and again, with labor-intensive early-intervention strategies and expensive remedial reading programs. Despite those interventions and Special Ed accommodations, reading and writing problems seem more pervasive than ever.

As things stand, we might fairly restate the education "facts of life" this way: We know reading comprehension and writing are hard for a significant number of students, and since text is our central tool in school, then lots of school failure seems unfortunate but unavoidable. And so do the myriad costly problems, educational and social, that flow from school failure.

HEEDING THE MESSAGE OF RELUCTANT READERS AND WRITERS

In trying to explain why students are disengaged from reading and writing, adults often cite competition with TV or digital media as the problem. Yet there was plenty of evidence of text as a learning problem in the one-room schoolhouse, where it was commonly accepted that some folks were good at "book learning" and others just weren't. In a world that needed lots of farmers, and then factory workers, text problems sorted themselves out: The text-smart stayed in school; the text-slow went to work. As a popular eighth-grade teacher nearing retirement told me, "Teaching used to be easier. When the boot factory was open, we all expected half the class to get good jobs right here in town, so nobody worried too much about college." It is only in a world where we expect all students to be text-proficient that the difficulty posed by text for a significant number of learners becomes a serious, costly education problem.

But what if the explanation for many reluctant readers and writers starts in our own classrooms? What if kids' disengagement with learning is a straightforward message to adults about how hard learning through text is? I received the following e-mail from an experienced high school Language Arts teacher who had seen an introductory storyboard workshop and decided to try it in her classroom: "It's SO cool to see students who have done next to nothing in my class all year create their storyboards!!!"

Those exclamation points only hint at how exciting it is to witness sudden engagement from students we thought we couldn't reach. Her stalled students demonstrated, in practical hands-on terms, that they were ready to engage with text when they saw a way in. Students who had done "next to nothing" were able to use storyboards to write because they provided a way to get ideas on paper, to brainstorm, organize, and revise—without requiring students to write exacting, difficult text from the start.

A Practical How-To

The good news from the back row is that your text-stalled students are ready to show you how to break the text-only learning trap that snares both students and teachers. Examining students' breakthroughs can help us recognize the two critical parts of the message students are sending:

- What makes text too hard for many learners?
- How do visual/verbal tools create a clear, effective bridge to text skills?

In chapters to come, we'll see the results of experiments in many class-rooms—we'll see improvements in reading comprehension and reluctant writers using text to create amazing stories. We'll examine students' breakthroughs to see what works for learners, and we'll see why "different" low-text tools make reading and writing easier and more meaningful for many students.

Chapter 2

Reluctant Writers Engage: Shared Writing

Working with a great teacher, I learned a lot about reluctant writers, about why they resist writing and how they can suddenly become engaged.

The first year I visited Linda Rief's classroom I already knew she was an accomplished writing teacher and an author of several books on writing with adolescents. Her focus is on meeting kids where they are, offering lots of choices for reading and writing. She was curious about drawing as a writing tool, but it was clear she had plenty of tools already. As I showed her kids how to build a story with stick pictures, they were tuned in; her experienced writers easily got the parallels with Linda's writer's workshop process, from brainstorming to conferencing to revising. As I gave them homework, to make a first-draft storyboard of a family story, the kids seemed excited. I hoped they'd show Mrs. Rief that this was more than just another prewriting strategy.

On day two we tried Shared Writing: building stories in a lively group process where students share stories from their storyboards before they write. Sharing went well; there was plenty of laughter at dumb pictures and helpful suggestions for revising stories.

One student told us how she broke her leg jumping off the garage roof with an umbrella for a parachute. Everyone liked her story, but her audience wanted more. They probed by asking questions. When we learned her older brother had encouraged her flying experiment, everyone recommended she add squares depicting how he manipulated her into jumping. She came back and told a second-draft storyboard that included the answers to questions she'd been asked.

The Shared Writing process emphasizes the writer-audience connection. Using telling-boards as the visual focus for this group-writing process, each writer tells his or her story and then shares it while listeners point out what they liked, ask questions, and offer suggestions. The writer then revises the storyboard and retells it until he or she has the story as complete as possible before writing the text. The process went: draw, tell, conference, revise, retell. We'll see in the research to come why telling is an important writing/thinking tool that—combined with drawing—can help break the text block.

A student tells her story to the class from an enlarged storyboard (original at right).

RELUCTANT WRITERS EVERYWHERE

I thought the sharing was going great until I realized a group of kids had quietly disengaged. When I asked a girl, slumped with arms crossed, what she thought of another student's story, she looked surprised I'd noticed her. Her nervous glance at other slouchers (to be sure she didn't have anything to contribute) was the tip-off—I'd found a support group common to many classrooms— the Reluctant Writers Club.

I'd seen reluctant writers set a tone of general resistance in classrooms— but these kids seemed out of step, almost sad. I could tell everyone was surprised when several hard-core club members dramatically broke ranks, volunteering to share their storyboards with the whole class. And they had solid stories. After hearing class reactions, they revised their work and shared a second draft that incorporated conferencing suggestions. As I was packing up, Linda seemed pleased with the results, but I was frustrated. I asked her about the kids who had opted out. I confessed I was surprised to find a group of reluctant writers in her room where kids wrote about what they cared about and received lots of support. I asked why she thought they didn't participate.

Her answer was straightforward; she didn't make excuses, or tell me what was "wrong" with "those kids." She told me, with real sadness, "I don't know what to do: If I give them freedom, they flounder; if I try to push them, they balk."

That day I was struck by her personal sense of failure as a teacher, stemming from her inability to engage all her kids as writers. Of course I'd failed to connect too, but I'd seen just enough breakthroughs to think this wasn't a personal problem; this was about text blocking kids. Without thinking, I blurted out, "Invite me back—I'll bet I can get all those kids to write." Linda looked at me skeptically before she grinned broadly, and said, "You're on." We agreed I could focus our experiment a little—the next time I came to her room, I'd push her reluctant writers; I'd get every student to really write.

Shane Won't Write

When I arrived to set up with a new class, Linda reminded me of our bet, smiled knowingly, and said, "Shane will be your challenge. I'm afraid even you  won't be able to get him to write." As I introduced story-boards, Shane was easy to spot—the boy in the back who sat up, yawned, and looked at me with studied disinterest before he laid his head on his desk and closed his eyes. Right from the start, Shane wanted me to know where he stood on writing.

We did Shared Writing again, but this time I made a point of saying, "With the Shared Writing process, the less text you write, the better text-writing you get." That idea, that drawing and telling are the easy way to build a story, got the attention of several reluctant writers. They bit early on, and several told showstopper stories that got everyone going. Everyone but Shane. Once I caught him lifting his head to hear a girl tell her grandfather's World War II story—about his submarine's crash dive while under attack by a bomber. Somehow a sailor was left on deck. Pointing to a square showing the guy pounding on the hatch with a wrench, she explained they had to decide whether to leave the sailor on deck or resurface and maybe all die. An irresistible story.

By the third day, when I had to leave, we'd all seen a number of stories go from brainstorming through conferencing and to storyboard revision. There was one last step in the process, the transition from storyboard to text—the "real writing." That transition is pretty straightforward; kids essentially transcribe their practiced telling into text, and Linda thought kids could handle that step, no problem. As I left, Shane, who hadn't said a word, gave me a slight nod good-bye.

Results—Yes and No

A couple of weeks later, Linda called to give me a rundown on the kids' work since I had left. She was excited, saying the results were great. Students had been expected to use their final draft storyboards to write text, but in keeping with her open approach, students could choose from a wide range of formats for their finished piece, from text-spare comics to text-only essays.

She said there was lots of good writing, including exciting visual work from some of her best writers and breakthrough pieces from her reluctant writers. But she ended by saying, "You got everybody writing, but you didn't get to Shane. He didn't storyboard. He did nothing."

She was sad, but matter-of-fact. I was disappointed too. I'd really thought Shane would somehow rise to the occasion, that the excitement of shared writing, being part of a community writing process, was irresistible. But what did I know about Shane? I confess I started to try to "explain" his behavior to myself in a way that must have been the way Linda felt. We had both missed connecting. I thought, "No matter what you do, some kids can't be reached."

WHAT HAS SHANE DONE?

About three weeks later, Linda called. She said, "I wanted to tell you what happened with Shane. Yesterday, I went over and sat with him. I told him I was frustrated and saddened that he hadn't done any work in my class all year. I told him I didn't know what else to do; he hadn't been interested in anything. He hadn't done anything. Then I told him I felt bad, but he was going to fail the class."

That's when Shane said, "But I have done something, Mrs. Rief." He reached into his notebook and pulled out a storyboard. It was a family story. Shane told her, using his storyboard, about his grandfather's escape from the Ayatollah Khomeini in Iran.

Shane's first-draft storyboard

With Linda's questions and suggestions, Shane expanded his storyboard through several more drafts, and then he transitioned to text. All text. You'll remember that to fulfill the assignment Shane could have gone "text-lite," made a comic, but Linda found Shane was determined to go for pure text, two full pages—far more than he had written all year. His grandfather's escape from Iran— why and how he escaped—was a compelling story that Shane was proud to tell.

RESEARCH: THE BRIDGE TO TEXT

Shortly after that call, I went to see Linda. We sat on the stairs near her classroom to talk about Shane. Despite seeing his breakthrough, she couldn't make sense of it. She raised questions I've heard many times before from teachers who've seen similar breakthroughs. The questions boiled down to these:

1. "Why wouldn't Shane write before now?"

2. "If Shane *wants* to write, why draw first?"

That day, all I could say for sure was that Shane's response to drawing was not unique; it fit a clear pattern I'd seen in many settings and across all grade levels. Now, with Linda's help, and with the research her colleague Donald Graves had conducted, I know there are compelling answers to teachers' questions about drawing as a writing tool, answers that resonate because they grow from kids' hard-won learning experiences.

Shane's *Other Story*

We can start with Shane's work—his first-draft storyboard—to find answers. Like any piece of honest writing, it can tell us a lot about its author. His board is a loose summary of his grandfather's escape from Iran. Until we hear Shane's full verbal telling, we can't know everything he has to say, but we can get a feel for his story.

We see Shane's story starts long ago in Iran and ends in the present. Look at his last square—the picture of his grandfather (once a penniless refugee) now standing by a full bookcase, with key words in the form of a headline— "VERY SUCCESSFUL WRITER." That simple stick-pic, like a formal family portrait posed with significant objects, speaks volumes. Shane tells us (consciously or unconsciously), "In my family, writing is *important*. Writing well is a sure sign of intelligence and of accomplishment."

I'm pretty sure that picture holds a school story all his teachers need to know. I'm guessing Shane, like many reluctant writers I've met, thinks of writing as something too important to do badly. We can guess he has failed at text many times before. Now, in eighth grade, he feels doomed; he

Shane's final square, an essay on the importance of writing

has nothing to say, especially in a class with a teacher like Mrs. Rief, who really cares about writing, who really wants to help. Shane has calculated the pain of writing poorly and decided he'd rather be seen as a lazy goof-up than a true failure: a bad writer.

Ironically, Shane (like many hard-core reluctant writers I've worked with) *values writing too much.* Contrary to their slouching, I-don't-care veneer, these students suffer from long-held, painful writer's block. This is one of the most common side effects of a text-only focus—kids stalled by text come to think they have nothing to say. Add adults' well-intentioned efforts to celebrate writing as *very important*, and the results make failure too costly. With the best intentions, we set the writing bar too high for lots of learners.

Drawing and Telling: Bridge to Text

But our experience with many breakthroughs with older students shows that blocked-by-text is only half of Shane's story. That brings us to Linda's second question, "Why does Shane want to draw before he will write?"

Donald Graves, a literacy researcher and teacher of writing, stumbled on the answer while observing young students learning to write. Graves repeatedly saw kids drawing before they would write. His breakthrough came in discovering that kids were using drawing as a natural path to writing.

Graves came to see drawing as kids' first on-paper thinking tool—a way of getting ideas on paper, organizing and growing them. When he saw kids telling a story out loud from their pictures, then putting the same words on paper in text, Graves realized kids were using their natural drawing skills in concert with telling

to build an effective bridge to text skills. Describing a young student's writing process, Graves wrote, "Drawing is the driving force behind much of Toni's writing. It serves as a rehearsal for the text as well as an important bridge from speech to print" (1984, p. 85).

Shane's sudden engagement with drawing seems less mysterious when we recognize this natural path to writing. And his use of drawing in the older classroom seems less strange when we recognize with Graves that drawing is a thinking/writing tool that can be used at any age. Describing the mechanics of kids' draw-and-tell-to-write process, Graves says, "The drawing, the hieroglyph, is an intermediary between oral and written discourse. At the same time, it should not be seen as something a child will outgrow. Pictorial representation continues to be a valuable tool for externalizing thought into adult-hood—as such professionals as physicians, engineers, and writers will attest" (1989, p. 14).

Having seen what can happen when drawing appears in the older classroom, let's let Linda tell us how these visual-verbal tools have evolved and changed the learning landscape in her classroom.

Chapter 3

Storyboards: More Than Stories

by Linda Rief

Recently, I was babysitting our two grandsons, Hunter, eight years old, and Harrison, six years old. I asked Hunter if there was any homework he needed to do before we read books together. He showed me what he had done, and we finished a math sheet together. I noticed he had put a "Free Homework Pass" over one page. It was over a writing assignment.

"Hunter, why did you put a homework pass over the writing?"

"Oh, I don't like writing, Grammy."

I was devastated but maintained a casual demeanor. "You don't like writing. . . . That's too bad. What don't you like about it?"

"Grammy, it's . . . so quiet."

"What do you mean?" I asked.

"It's so hard. You have to think all by yourself, and it's so quiet."

We proceeded to have a writing conference. I asked Hunter what he was supposed to do, and told him that maybe if we worked together he wouldn't have to use up that one homework pass. He had to write an ending to *Humpty Dumpty*. He came up with suggestions, which I wrote down for him, exactly the way he said them. Sometimes I drew quick stick figures and key words, other times I wrote down his exact words. (In retrospect, I wish I had drawn everything he said, just to see if that would change this third grader's opinion about writing by getting words on paper in a more palatable way.)

In his ending, he had Humpty Dumpty fall a number of times, with the king's men always putting him together again. But, by the time he was ready to finish the story, he said, "I don't think they want to glue him together again!"

"So what will happen? What will they do?"

His ending?

"Glue him again?" said the king's men. "Forget it."
So they scraped him all up, and ate him for lunch.

As Hunter wrote the ending, he kept saying it aloud. He said, "Forget it," several times, and finally said, "Forget it—that needs an exclamation point." He inserted one. When he was done, he read it aloud and smiled. "I like this," he said. "Thanks, Grammy." He put the free homework pass back on the calendar, to cover another assignment more painful than writing, one hopes.

DRAWING AS A THINKING TOOL

Hunter's "It's so quiet. . . . It's so hard. You have to think it up yourself," keeps ringing in my ears. He had an idea. He just needed to talk it out, to hear it out loud. Storyboarding might have helped him see it, once he talked it out, but he didn't have either tool. He chose to take the pass. If that's the experience many of my eighth graders have had, no wonder they choose to not even attempt the writing. *The cost is too high*, as Roger says, *to do it badly*. Was I putting too much emphasis on writing, without giving the kids the tools to do it well enough to want to do it at all?

No matter how hard I worked at trying to get all kids to write, I never understood why a couple of kids in every class refused to participate. Is it that they *can't* write? Or *won't* write? Why? What was I doing wrong? I heard Roger Essley speak at a conference. He was speaking about his dyslexia and difficulty with writing throughout his schooling. Teachers wouldn't let him draw, yet it was through pictures that he represented all he understood or was trying to understand. He talked about *drawing as thinking* (stick figures and key words), not *drawing as performance* (creating a piece of art). I listened hard. I had used pictures and students' drawing to inspire writing, but I had never thought about drawing as thinking, where *drawing didn't count*, and *spelling didn't count*. I sat up and listened harder. He seemed to be talking about first-draft thinking. What if kids were encouraged to represent what they wanted to say, what they were thinking, through stick figures and key words?

I remembered an article I had read by Judith Fueyo. In it she says, ". . . as language arts teachers we are after words, oral and written, but need they be the exclusive avenue by which we arrive at words? . . . Einstein admitted that he did not think in words, but visual images. His early formulations for the theory of relativity came in images of himself riding a light wave. Only later did he come to words" (1991, p. 13).

I thought about all the research I had read about reading, and how good readers get visual images in their heads as they construct meaning from their reading. The kids who didn't write also told me they hated reading.

They told me they saw nothing when they read. Did they also "see nothing" when they tried to write? What if students who struggled with writing were invited to use visual tools to tell their stories? Would that help all kids come more easily to words? Would that also help them as readers, if they were invited to draw? Encouraged to draw?

I thought about the first story Nancie Atwell tells in her first edition of *In the Middle*—the story of her frustration with Jeff, who spent most of his time drawing. How she resorted to telling him to "stop drawing, and get to work," even though his drawing led to a multitude of writing. Jeff finally told Nancie one day, "Listen, Ms. Atwell. This is the way I do it, the way I write. As long as I get it done, what do you care?" (1987, p. 7).

It wasn't until Nancie saw Donald Graves' research demonstrating that drawing and telling are natural writing tools that she recognized she had missed what Jeff could teach her. I found myself wondering if I, too, had students like Jeff. Had I missed something?

Is drawing the way some students need to come to writing? Is it a tool we dismiss too easily, especially in upper grades? Is it a tool for more than struggling writers, but for any person, even a gifted writer as he or she tries to convey ideas, as in Einstein's case?

I invited Roger to my classroom. I watched as he modeled Shared Writing (described in the previous chapter). I saw how easily students used stick figures and key words to construct their stories. And I saw how, using tellingboards, they could easily add, delete, or move squares around to tell the story in a better way, based on their audience's reactions. When the tellingboard is complete, it serves as a guide for the student to use in his or her writing.

I was amazed. Kids who had never written before began writing, aided by pictures to guide them. And even the most reluctant of writers began to produce.

Shane was the biggest surprise. He had written nothing for six months, until Roger introduced tellingboards. As Roger explained, Shane told and wrote the story of his grandfather's escape from Iran under the Ayatollah Khomeini. It was his first piece of writing for the entire year. He added to his story with each succeeding draft, until he had enough visuals in front of him to let him *see* and tell his story.

The experience with Shane and drawing turned out to be the tip of the iceberg. The Shared Writing produced many exciting breakthroughs with students I had struggled to reach. The original intent was to introduce kids to a strategy or tool for getting their writing ideas onto paper and eventually into words. Over time the power of drawing became undeniable, and I found drawing as a thinking tool and the shared writing becoming an integral part of my classroom for writing, reading, and note-taking.

SIMPLIFYING CONFERENCES

I also noticed that the processes of drawing and sharing the writing served to simplify conferences and revision. Megan was a good writer, but she was reluctant to revise her writing. It seemed like too much work to have to add information or to move information around. But with the tellingboard, she could do that without having to produce a rewritten second draft. The pictures made revision easier. She didn't have to add paragraph after paragraph and go through the tedious process of moving all those words around, until she had the pictures complete and in the order in which she wanted to tell the story.

Look at Megan's first and second drafts of writing as tellingboards, where she is telling the story about her dog that ate $100 and how her dad insisted they had to recover the money through "poop patrol." Notice how the second draft became much richer through Shared Writing, before she went to the written draft. Megan is able to better develop character roles and add humor by describing her characters through their appearance, thoughts, and dialogue.

Megan's first draft

She is also able to organize the story into distinct sections with related action squares, including an introduction to the dog's unsavory eating habits and the money-cleaning process. After an additional editing conference, in which we went through and corrected the conventions of language in her first text draft, she submitted her final draft, shown on page 36.

Megan's second draft

$100 . . . Gone in Five Gulps

Who would think that your bank deposit could be gone in five gulps? Well, my mom and dad definitely didn't!

It was a school night, and my parents were just tucking in my brother and sister. I was just heading upstairs for bed when I heard a few crashes and the sound of two paws hitting the floor. I went back downstairs to find bunches of loose paper and money all over the floor. The second I saw this I knew that my dog, Jesse, probably ate something, because ever since she was a puppy she loved to eat paper. Once I actually had to use the excuse, "My dog ate my homework!" It was the truth.

I called my parents down, and believe me, they weren't too happy when they saw this! "Martha, why did you leave the money at the end of the desk?" my father asked. "How was I supposed to know she would eat it?!" my mom replied back. It was actually a little funny listening to them. My parents put my dog in her kennel, picked up the money, and counted what was there to see if we had everything. We were one hundred dollars short.

In the morning when we had the whole family together my dad announced that we would be on "poop patrol" for the next week. The whole neighborhood found this pretty humorous, considering my dad is a veterinarian. It was my mom's turn to walk Jesse first, and she lucked out because the dog didn't have to go. My brother, sister, and I took turns walking Jesse also, but she never went to the bathroom when we were walking her. My dad was the "lucky" one.

"I found it!" my dad exclaimed, as he ran into the house and grabbed a bucket and surgical gloves. He went back outside, and started to pick the money, bit by bit, out of the poop. On two of the bills there was a corner missing so he had to search extra hard to find them. Relieved that we had finally found the hundred dollars, we went outside and laid the bills out on a paper towel (covering our noses at the same time). Twenty, forty, sixty, eighty . . . we were missing one! We needed one more twenty! So my dad searched through the poop very carefully one more time but had no luck, so this meant that "poop patrol" was on for one more day.

We eventually found the last twenty and laid it out with the others. Three of the twenties were swallowed whole, and the other two each had a corner ripped off, which we somehow managed to find.

The next thing we had to do was clean them off. We filled a bowl with hot water and soap and let the bills soak until we thought it was safe to take them out. We let them dry, and then taped the pieces that had been torn off. They almost looked as good as new!

We took the money to the bank and explained to the clerk why we needed an exchange. She was amused by our story, even though I'm not sure she believed it. She was more than happy to exchange the money for us. Whenever we go to that bank, she just looks at us and starts to laugh.

Since Jesse ate the one hundred dollars she has consumed fifteen dollars. That's all the money she has eaten. She still does eat practically everything in sight, including two pecan pies (Thanksgiving), a basket of Dove chocolate (Easter), tons of tissues (mostly used), six candles (they were mine!), plus so much more. Not ONCE has she had an upset stomach or even been slightly sick! Despite all this, we still love her.

I began to realize how much faster conferences went if students used a tellingboard to share their stories with peers before they began writing. The answers to questions and the addition or deletion of suggestions helped them revise the content. The response to the tellingboards was the same as in writing conferences, but it went so much faster. Peers confirmed what each student did well, asked questions, and gave a suggestion. Look at how much easier conferences become if the writer can add short notes in small boxes that are placed in the spot where that information is most appropriate. The tellingboard provides a visible way of showing how to organize the writing.

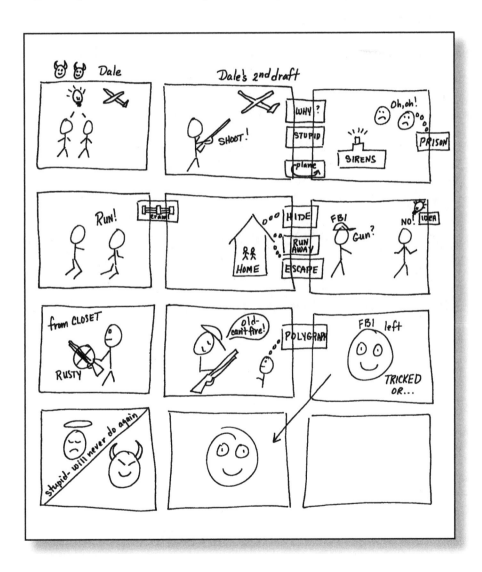

Dale struggled when it came to figuring out where to add information that came from questions or suggestions. But his revision choices became much clearer when he placed small boxes containing questions and one-word comments at the exact places on his board where he needed to address them in the story.

Final Draft as Writing or as a Cartoon

I also want to give students the option of writing their final draft as a cartoon, if that format effectively conveys all they want to get across with their story. Dan interviewed his dad, who willingly told him the story of the "stupidest" thing he had ever done. Dan had not done a lot of writing previously. This was one of the first stories he told. He relished the reaction from peers when they enthusiastically responded to his first drafts.

As juniors in high school, Dan's dad and a buddy decided to swipe a weather balloon and a hydrogen tank from the chemistry lab, after hearing the teacher talk about how dangerous and explosive hydrogen was. Dan humorously described the reasoning of these nerdy young men, using caricatures to show how the teens were intellectually smart, but had little common sense. The cartoon captured the story well, and had eighth graders shaking their heads in disbelief, but also relating "stupid" things they had tried, even though they knew better.

Dan's humor is revealed in his illustrations, which lay the groundwork for his storytelling.

Drawing Understanding From Reading Through Note-Taking

Because tellingboards helped so many students find success as writers, I wondered how using *drawing as thinking* might help kids better understand what they read: whether it's used to depict a short story or a poem in one frame; to take notes on a difficult text, such as those used in social studies; or to show understandings of characters or themes from a movie, play, or novel.

While students were viewing the film *The Wave*—the story of a history lesson about group control that went awry in a high school classroom in Palo Alto, California, in the 1960s—I wondered if students could answer several questions about the Holocaust if each one followed a different character throughout the movie. The questions were:

- How can peer pressure usurp individual rights?
- When does dedication to the group cross the line from good judgment to blind loyalty and fanaticism?
- How could 11 million people be murdered while the world turned its back and said it didn't know?

I had each student follow one of several characters by drawing the actions of the characters, so we could figure out what choices each made and the motivation that guided or misguided those choices.

As Michelle watches *The Wave*, she follows one of the main characters, Robert.

After the movie, I grouped the students by character, and had them share their drawings as they discussed why a given character had acted a particular way. When the students shared their findings as a whole class, it led to the richest discussions, because the students had gained a much better understanding of each character from their drawings. Each student then returned to the original questions I posed at the outset, and using the ideas from their drawings and discussion, were able to write an independent response with a clear main idea and substantial examples.

I think sometimes we ask too much of students when we expect them to keep track of all the characters and themes in a movie or novel. By asking them to pay attention—which they did with great intensity—to one particular character, they garnered a far deeper understanding of that character. The discussion and writing that followed their note-gathering furthered their comprehension of the movie. It was the drawing that enabled them to notice, capture, and talk about choices the characters made so they could answer the questions I posed to them.

ANALYZING CHARACTER

Although the example I have given you is based on a film, the same technique works with some short stories, personal narratives, and memoirs. Students draw to follow and analyze a character; they draw summaries of a more difficult story in order to follow the plot; or they can look at metaphorical and vivid language through the images created in their heads and explore how these images might help them make inferences about the text's theme or message.

After I shared my findings about drawing as thinking with other teachers and discussed how positively it affected my students' analysis of characters from *The Wave*, Jennifer Wheet, a high school teacher, sent me an exercise she created that her juniors had used to analyze the characters in *Macbeth*. This technique could be done with any play or novel, especially ones with multiple characters. After following their chosen character and drawing their findings, the students used the tellingboard as an outline, or points of proof, for their written assignment. Jennifer said they were the best character-analysis papers she had ever received.

Sample character-analysis storyboard for *Macbeth*

I used Jennifer's design with *Macbeth* to help my students better understand the characters' choices and motivational drives in *Romeo and Juliet*. After color-coding the members of each family (blue for the Montagues and red for the Capulets), we then construct a tellingboard that allows students to represent graphically how the characters fit into one family or the other. Each class constructs its own master sheet, showing how the characters are related to each other, with a hint of personality traits, through each drawing. As we watch clips of the Zefferelli version of *Romeo and Juliet* and read many of the scenes, students are prepared to follow one character with the analysis sheet I have constructed for them.

Cast of characters: *Romeo and Juliet*

Tellingboard—Character Analysis for *Romeo and Juliet*

Each day, I give the students time to draw the actions of their character. I ask them to put into their own words how they know that a character has done a particular thing, or I ask them to find Shakespeare's words in the play to support the character's choices.

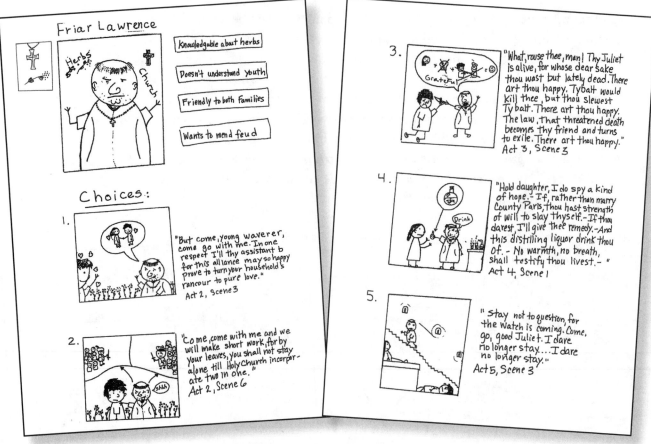

Character analysis of Friar Lawrence

At the end of the reading and viewing, students gather by character, talk out their findings, and then write a monologue from their character's viewpoint that justifies or reconsiders his or her choices. They write the monologue alone or collaboratively—then decide how to deliver it. Like Jennifer, since I have used drawing to help my students capture all they read and view, I notice their analysis of characters and their choices are much more thoughtful and thorough.

I have only begun to tap the surface of this iceberg. I thought, if students are able to follow and capture so much more as we read difficult literature, what would happen if they were given this tool in other classes? How much do they understand? How much do they understand but can't convey through words?

UNDERSTANDING DRAWN FROM OTHER DISCIPLINES

The social studies teacher told me Tad seemed to understand very little of anything he read, no matter how simple the text. He gave me a typical worksheet filled with five paragraphs of writing: "Reasons for the American Revolution."

I gave Tad a sheet with five large squares on it and told him to draw what he understood (the main idea) as I read each paragraph aloud to him. We did all five. I read, he drew. Then he explained each drawing to me. Here is the first paragraph from the worksheet and Tad's drawn and oral response.

England used a plan known as mercantilism to keep it rich and strong. According to this plan, a country becomes rich by selling more goods to other countries than it buys from them. England applied this plan to the American colonies. It passed many laws forcing the colonies to buy goods only from England. Americans could not trade directly with any other country. The American colonies came to depend on England for everything. Mercantilism thus prevented the American colonies from becoming as strong and as rich as they might have been.

Pointing to his drawing, Tad said: "The colonists are being made to pay high prices to England because they can only trade with them. England is more powerful. That's why they're bigger. This was mercantilism."

Tad was equally clear in his understanding of all five paragraphs. He knows a lot, but he can't seem to get those understandings down in writing. If we are serious about differentiated instruction, shouldn't drawing be a tool that all kids are offered? I am not suggesting this was a comprehensive study, but it is an area that deserves a lot more attention. Every teacher is a teacher of reading. We all need to look more carefully at the range of tools we are giving kids to access and show all they understand from the texts we assign them.

At a workshop I was giving last year in Toronto, a teacher handed me the following drawing at the end of the day. He said it was all he remembered from his schooling 50 years earlier, but the memory was still vivid and strong. His teacher was trying to teach students the meaning and pronunciation for the word *onomatopoeia*, and drew the following on the board.

All he remembered from his schooling 50 years earlier. The information stayed in his head because he could still *see* the drawing. I think we could be taking drawing as thinking more seriously in our classrooms as we work with all kids. It may be the best tool they have for showing us all they know and understand. If we want all kids to be thoughtful, articulate, responsible citizens of the world, they have to be good readers and writers. And to reach that goal, we have to offer them every tool available. I don't want Hunter or any other third graders (*or* eighth graders) to put free homework passes over their writing because it's "so quiet."

Chapter 4

Visual Tools for Differentiated Instruction

L inda Rief opens her chapter discussing her grandson's difficult experience with a writing assignment in third grade. He says, "It's so hard. You have to think all by yourself, and it's so quiet." I know too many kids share his experience of being cut off by the push to literacy.

When I was in third grade, I liked the story of Cinderella. As a student at the bottom of the literacy pile, I could have used a Fairy Godmother. I dreamed, along with everyone else toiling in the back row, that we might somehow magically get smarter. Now I've seen magic performed in a third-grade classroom. I've seen the Fairy Godmother turn a literacy frog into a prince simply by redesigning a lowly worksheet.

In this chapter, we'll see that dramatic transformation, and we'll peek behind the curtain to see how a teacher can transform learning with the most mundane tools. This teacher will show how a small change in practice can make practical differentiated instruction an instant reality in the classroom. Indeed, we'll examine the goals of differentiation and show why simple drawing should be a classroom essential if we hope to offer all our learners a way into the literacy circle.

TAPPING VISUAL SKILLS

Amy Levy Rocci was an early collaborator in my visual-tools work. She and I experimented with storyboards as a writing tool in her third-grade classroom, and we would meet occasionally and compare notes. She would tell me about her third graders' drawing and writing breakthroughs, and I'd share similar anecdotes about what I'd seen with kids in other grades.

Often in our conversations, I would express frustration with classroom practices I thought blocked kids. Amy listened, patient with my views. Sometimes she explained the classroom reality to me, detailing the stress of balancing the

competing demands of curriculum and time. But one day, when I commented on how few visual tools teachers offer kids, Amy got really frustrated. She said, "You don't see all the visual tools, the graphic organizers, we use. Those are all *visual tools*."

I was taken aback. Amy handed me a sheet saying, "There are lots of these available—if you look. Some are better than others. This is one I like."

As I scanned her visual organizer, I had a nasty shock of recognition. Below a "Fairy Tales" headline was a series of questions running down the page, with lines provided for the students to write answers. "Oh, I hate these!" I blurted out. After we both laughed, I tried to explain.

I told her my son Andy, a weak reader and writer in the early grades, had visual organizers just like this for homework. He tried on his own, and then, frustrated, he'd come to me. Often he didn't understand the questions or the instructions he was supposed to follow. As we read and sorted things out, he became restless, then resistant. When he finally got to writing, his weak text skills made his short answers sound awkward, even to him. By the time we were done, we were both worn out, and he felt defeated.

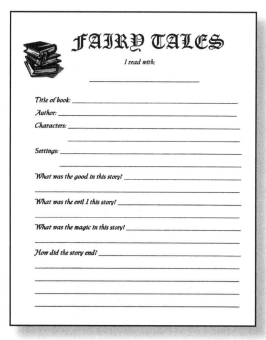

Amy's sample "visual organizer"

What Is "Visual" Learning?

Amy listened. She was sympathetic, and she acknowledged Andy was not alone in his struggles. Still, she explained that visual organizers like this were carefully designed to accomplish a series of essential third-grade literacy tasks. In this case, the students learn to recognize basic story construction, plot, characters, and so forth. The worksheet was a hands-on way to let kids review and reinforce class content.

I wondered aloud what made this sheet a visual tool. I was honestly baffled. We looked together, viewing the organizer from a struggling reader's point of view. As we tried to see how this "carefully designed" sheet might help kids struggling with text, Amy understood how the organizer might actually block her kids. Finally she said, "There has to be a better way to do this."

Amy had seen how storyboards with drawing could break the text block for her writers. She suggested a visual-learning experiment. She would try to modify her fairy tale worksheet to make it more accessible to weak readers and writers.

How Text Blocks

Before we look at Amy's true visual tool, let's turn back to page 45 and look at this so-called visual organizer the way a third-grade emerging reader and reluctant writer might. We'll also keep Amy's literacy/curriculum goals in mind: to review and reinforce class content and assess each student's learning. I hope you'll see that the central flaw here—using text-in and text-out materials, organizer or not—creates learning problems for students and teachers alike.

The first thing kids see, scanning the whole page, is the big "Fairy Tales" title with typed questions down the page and empty lines for text answers. It's clear that this is an all-text format—no pictures to help: We will read, then we will write.

If I'm a poor decoder, all these lines of text look essentially the same to me. This format gives no visual clues, no context or layout variation to help me understand what the questions are about. For example, no questions are grouped together to suggest a linkage.

To a child with weak text skills, this sheet looks like a series of text hurdles with the last one a showstopper: all those empty lines. Kids know what they mean: "Please give your answers in text alone." In short, for many kids, just starting the sheet is a painful invitation to work with little payoff. They will work hard and look dumb.

Text tools are, by nature, narrowly focused on a specific set of learning skills. Ask yourself, why do most third-grade tools sold as visual organizers have little visual content? We're not talking about adding cute illustrations to the page to make it look inviting. Clip art of dancing pigs or butterflies, common on many organizers, are visual, but they are not helpful. Images that don't reinforce content can actually confuse learners. I've seen disconnected pictures, or poor sequencing of content, mislead learners with false clues about the task at hand.

Visual Informs Learners

Here is Amy's redesigned worksheet—a true visual tool.

The first thing her kids see is a storyboard format—lots of boxes, with both text and pictures. But this sheet looks different from the storyboard grids they've seen before. It is divided into three parts: two boxes across the top, six connected boxes in the middle, and three more boxes at the bottom.

The format is Amy's central innovation, and it's a big one. This sheet is truly *visual*, designed to display information in a meaningful way. It helps kids understand and think through the task ahead. Immediately, kids can see there are three distinct sections to consider, and they can guess by the connected boxes in each group that these are related concepts. This three-part format was designed to reinforce the literacy lesson discussed in class, "We

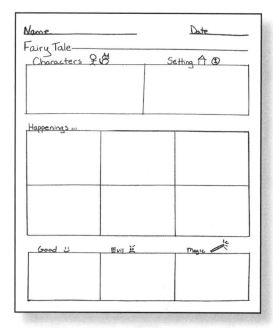

Amy's new, authentic visual organizer reinforces content and allows diverse responses.

will divide a magic story's content into three distinct categories." This is not a list of questions where every line looks equal—and that makes a world of difference. *This visual sheet informs before it asks kids to perform.*

Now let's look at those three parts. What can we learn about the literacy task at hand?

■ The top two boxes are for setting and characters; each box has a word and a symbol. Even children who are preliterate can remember what goes in there. And kids know these two categories are related, but different from what comes next.

■ The middle section, six connected boxes, is immediately recognizable to the kids as a six-square storyboard. They know that's how we retell a story here.

■ The bottom three boxes ask three questions specific to a magic fairy tale: What's good? What's evil? And what's the magic in the story? These are the same words used in the original text worksheet, but notice that here, since they are not asked as full sentences, the questions seem less specific, less intimidating, less like they might have a single right answer that only the teacher knows.

Finally, this visual format sends one more essential message. The storyboard format implies that the teacher is not expecting text-only answers. The boxes invite all students, those who are text-confident and those who are text-phobic, to get to work.

VISUAL TOOLS ENGAGE ALL LEARNERS

Amy told her students to use the usual storyboarding rules: provide your answers through simple stick pictures and a few key words in each square. Since this was the first time her students had ever tried a storyboard worksheet for class content, she suggested they all look at the central six-square storytelling section. The students discussed what key words they might put in the first square to begin retelling the story. Everyone agreed to put in a picture and write the key words "work, work, work," as reflected in the sample at left.

Two students offer different work, from solid construction to dramatic points of view.

Now, let's see what kids made of this new writing tool. The first time I saw Amy's new storyboard organizer, we were presenting together at a conference. As Amy showed the worksheets projected on a screen, there was a buzz of excitement, folks leaning forward and examining her students' work. Amy told the audience that *everybody* in the class created a successful storyboard, a notable fact considering this was the first time her kids had seen or used a storyboard worksheet format.

It was obvious from the students' confident work that this new design was user-friendly. Anyone could see that the students' answers were presented in a way that communicated effectively. Their storyboards were easy for peers, the teacher, or parents to read. Several teachers commented on how expressive the work was. Some said that they were amazed at how varied kids' responses were to the story.

Amy said the range of the expression struck her, too. She was intrigued to find several of her "best writers" especially adept at telling a story in pictures and clearly enjoying the chance to perform at a more expansive level. She noted one girl's varied viewpoints, including a picture that showed Cinderella holding an invitation from a bird's eye perspective (see the storyboard at right on page 48).

A Literacy Frog Becomes a Prince

Amy said that for her, the most telling outcome of her experiment was the work of one boy. Mark was significantly behind in both reading and writing. His issues were severe enough that he usually had an aide to help him with text work. Mark had recently begged her, "Ms. Rocci, please, don't make me write." Yet when this storyboard worksheet was introduced, Mark asked for the sheet and the book and went to the back of the room by himself to work. A half hour later he came back with his completed sheet.

Amy put Mark's storyboard up on the overhead.

Mark's first storyboard worksheet shows what he knows.

The room was quiet as we looked at Mark's results. It was all there: the characters, the setting, the summary of the story, the good, bad, and the magic— all filled in. Pause here for a drum roll. . . . Mark did this all by himself.

Earlier I quoted Tomlinson saying teachers need to learn from their students how to differentiate. What can we learn by reading Mark's storyboard? At a glance we can see he can deconstruct and rebuild this story with ease. He has completed the basic content review independently, and that's remarkable. Amy says that using text alone, Mark can't tell us much, even with the help of an aide.

But he has a lot more to teach us about drawing as a writing/thinking tool. He deconstructs the story with style, and his drawings are both concise and detailed. Look at how effectively he creates a clear character code, each person distinctly different, presented with their text names. That's why he needed the book; he knew the teacher wanted the names, but he needed to copy some of that text.

After getting his characters and two settings—home and castle—established, Mark shifted into high gear telling the famous story in the six-square center section. In the first box, we see Cinderella scrubbing the floor with bubbles in the air all around her. This is effective visual storytelling. You'll note Mark did not use key words, but his bubbles are the visual equivalent of the key words "work, work, work." Mark is showing he can communicate effectively in pictures, but hang on to your hat, he is about to take us to the next level.

Look carefully at Box 2, the magic square. This is an extraordinary picture, worth several thousand words if we adults truly want an accurate assessment of what Mark knows and what he can do. Here he tells us how the Fairy Godmother makes her magic in the story. That's hard to do in one square—especially using Mark's rules: no extraneous words, please.

See what he has done! For those familiar with the meaning of symbols (the physics teacher or the engineer), this is a very sophisticated picture. Mark has created a simple visual equation that says, "To create magic you need one fairy godmother + one magic wand + several mice + a pumpkin + ..." Follow his symbols and see how this boy has taken a narrative story, and using picture writing in combination with a math concept, he has written a clear symbol equation that ends with "= a magic carriage" in the next square. Behold the magic formula in symbols for "bibbity, bobbity, boo."

In his full retelling, Mark uses only one key word—Cinderella on her way to the ball, says "Buy" meaning "Bye" (a common-sense spelling after my own heart). His no-text work is sending us a clear message: "I am a true reluctant writer. I can tell you what I know, communicate, and think on paper, but I cannot do it well in text alone, not yet." For sure, using that

one word, Mark made a "mistake"; trust me, it can be a very painful error if someone undermines his powerful communication with a dismissive "You spelled it wrong!" Fortunately, Mark understood from Amy's draw-to-show-what-you-know format that spelling and text were not the focus of the class task; communication was.

The focused silence of teachers examining Mark's work was exciting. Most teachers have little experience with drawing as a literacy tool, but I hoped they were seeing what students can communicate when we break the narrow bonds of text-only strategies. Mark's careful work shows he knows all about story elements and more; Mark shows he can summarize, organize, and communicate ideas on paper if we allow him to use his natural learning skills.

PRACTICAL DIFFERENTIATED INSTRUCTION

I was struck by Mark's work, and by the way Amy Rocci's choice of tools allowed Mark to be successful. Mark's breakthrough is a dramatic demonstration of how using drawing as a thinking/writing tool can transform the learning experience for kids left behind in a text-only curriculum. Mark said, "Don't make me write"—until he was offered drawing as a writing tool. Then he said, "Give me that!" Rocci's worksheet fundamentally changed the text-narrow learning equation: For the first time, Mark saw a real choice of writing tools, and a clear invitation to use his innate drawing and thinking skills. He stepped forward to transform himself from a self-perceived failure who needed an aide, into a self-sufficient success.

Tomlinson says teachers must learn from their students to differentiate, but she acknowledges that this can be tough, especially for new teachers. "Young teachers are developing the gross motor skills of teaching. Differentiation is a fine motor skill. The way to get there is to teach them to look at kids as individuals and to let kids show you what they can do. We want young teachers to develop the right set of habits that will lead to differentiation. In truth, differentiation probably calls for an expert teacher" (Hess, "Teachers Can Benefit").

Amy's experiment with drawing offers us exciting news. She recognized how tough it is to differentiate a text lesson using text-only tools. Drawing as a literacy tool gave her a unique opportunity to see what her students could do with learning choices.

But what can she learn from her students? She might focus on Mark's dramatic success as a sign that he needs an accommodation: drawing as an individual choice when the class is focused on text tasks. Yet the full meaning of Mark's individual breakthrough comes when we see his success in true context. His eager embrace of drawing as a writing tool was not a sign that he was a "different learner." Mark's success was echoed by all his peers; in their deft and varied work, we see how easily all learners embrace drawing with text. We also see that each student took the assignment where he or she wanted to go. Amy's experiment demonstrates that everyone benefited by opening the text-narrow door.

This is the hallmark of true differentiated instruction: offering learning choices that support and challenge all learners. Amy's new worksheet, with drawing as a central tool, engaged her struggling students in a way text alone cannot, and it inspired her best writers to try a wider range of expressive communication. Our students often have more knowledge and joy to share than they can convey in text alone. If we believe writing is about communicating, then offering our students time-tested writer's tools that do not require text mastery is providing them with a chance to write more easily and often, and to communicate more deeply.

Amy saw in her students' diverse and nuanced work that encouraging and supporting a diversity of learning styles does not require inventing endless choices for individual learners. Her students show us true diversity is most easily fostered by offering choices everyone can grasp and easily use. When we remember Donald Graves' finding that drawing is the first natural companion to text for *all* young learners, and their first on-paper thinking tool, Amy's students' embrace of drawing makes perfect sense. Adding drawing to the mix gave everyone a whole range of new choices and lots of room to grow.

Amy's worksheet is a practical differentiation tool beginners can use. Her drawing-with-text format offers an easy way for any beginning teacher to explore the fundamentals of differentiation with students without altering the curriculum or class literacy goals.

Similar experiments, by beginning and expert teachers alike, also show dramatic success with differentiated instruction. We might summarize the results as follows: If differentiated instruction aims at offering students authentic learning choices, and we find a third of our students can show us more of what they know using drawing as a writing-thinking tool (a very conservative estimate), then drawing is by definition a differentiation essential. In practical terms, this means the teacher who expands any text-narrow tool by adding drawing to a worksheet, test, journal, or essay is making differentiated instruction a reality for all learners from the get-go.

AUTHENTIC ASSESSMENT, TOO

Finally, a key goal of differentiation is developing assessment tools that accurately measure diverse students' progress. It is essential to note that Rocci's students' work in drawing offers learning data we can never access with an all-text assessment. Using drawing in assessment gives essential evidence, both about what students know and about how our students can best learn.

In a data-driven school climate, accurate assessment is critical for students and teachers. Without Mark's work in drawing, an administrator or parent, seeing Mark's inadequate text responses, might conclude Amy is failing as a teacher. With Mark's drawing it is easy to show that she is doing a fine job, and we know Mark can learn if we offer him visual tools. That's powerful data. Schools adding targeted storyboard/drawing to their assessment mix find they are instantly rewarded with more data and more accurate inclusive assessment of students, especially in early grades, where students' limited text skills hinder test responses.

In short, teaching students to use drawing as a thinking tool with text and considering their drawing work solid evidence of learning is, by definition, differentiation in assessment; and it is differentiation that makes the assessment more inclusive and more effective. Students and teachers all benefit when assessments begin to reflect a more expansive view of what learning data is valuable.

VISUAL TOOLS FOR MANY LITERACY TASKS

Amy's visual worksheet experiment shows how breaking narrow text boundaries pays big dividends for all learners. As we go forward you will see how easily storyboards can be adapted for a broad range of literacy tasks. You'll see many other formats teachers have created to increase reading comprehension, make note-taking easier and more memorable, organize and present classroom content, and write collaboratively.

In the next chapter, Amy shows how she weaves storyboards and drawing as a thinking tool into the fabric of her learners' day—creating a visual learning community.

Chapter 5

Developing a Storyboarding Classroom

by Amy Levy Rocci

When I began to teach third grade, I had been told that this was a pivotal year for kids. I had learned in school that this was the year when students are expected to "read to learn" instead of "learn to read." I learned in my classroom that this was not reality. I saw that for some students this transition is not easy, and the struggle with literacy really begins to affect them. I learned quickly that conventional tools had limited success, and I'd better have some practical strategies to help those who were having difficulty making this transition.

DIFFERENT LEARNING

I first met Roger Essley when his son was a student in my class, and he showed students how to write their own picture book from a family story. I'd never seen storyboards used as a writing tool, and watching students draw to build ideas was exciting. (I saw students who struggled with literacy motivated and excited about building their stories through drawing!) Our third-grade team found collecting and sharing family stories valuable, and we were all excited about the quality of the final product when each student created an elegant picture-book story.

Yet, as I reflected on the storyboard writing process and how it helped all my kids get to text, I had a feeling storyboards with drawing might be more than just a tool for making picture books. During the next school year, I started to experiment with storyboarding throughout the curriculum. This was the same year Mark, the student you heard about in the previous chapter, was in my room. It was no secret Mark was struggling. He was more than a year behind with literacy skills.

Due to these issues, a classroom assistant helped in supporting Mark's literacy development. A perfect example of Mark's difficulty in school due to his literacy struggles was that he did not have a problem with grade-level math unless he had to read the directions or decipher a word problem. The reading put up a roadblock. Mrs. S., the educational assistant working with me, took away the roadblock by reading to him. Similarly, in science and social studies, Mark learned the concepts and could convey them orally; the reading and writing got in the way. Once again, Mrs. S. helped by reading or acting as Mark's scribe.

Mark participated as best he could during our regular classroom program of reading and writing. He had told me more than once, "I can't read." This wasn't true, but it was Mark's way of letting me know that he felt he couldn't keep up with the rest of the class.

Having an adult bridge gaps for students so that they can succeed in the regular classroom is common in schools that value inclusive educational practice. But I had to wonder if Mark felt he was doing the same work as everyone else. Did Mark feel that the work was his? Did his peers see Mark as a regular member of the class? Certainly, I would choose this method of instruction over having Mark pulled out of my classroom to a resource room to receive instruction away from his peers, but I wondered if there was a way to help Mark to learn more independently and to do the same work as everyone else.

It was Mark who helped answer my questions, during our unit on fairy tales. We were starting a project of comparing Cinderella stories. I had stories from many countries as well as fun "spoof" stories based on the Cinderella theme. As you know from Roger's earlier recounting, I'd used a graphic organizer during this unit, to reinforce content and assess learning. With Roger's encouragement, for the first time I designed and tried using a more visual sheet, one that allowed students to use drawing as a thinking tool while making sure that I got the information I wanted. (See page 47.)

As you saw, that was an incredibly successful tool for Mark, and for the rest of my students. This new storyboard sheet was less dependent on text mastery and provided the opportunity for creativity for all students. It was clear that this activity, along with additional use of storyboards, bridged a gap for Mark; and he bridged it *independently*. Mark came up to me to ask for a copy of the book to help him spell the names. He then went back to his seat and got to work without asking for help, which provided an incredible boost to his self-esteem. Mark began to become a regular part of reading groups in the classroom. He began to feel comfortable enough to take his turn reading aloud and started to take more risks with writing on his own.

DIFFERENTIATE: GOING TO THE NEXT LEVEL

Students like Mark have taught me the importance of hands-on drawing as a thinking tool for many learners and for me as a teacher. I've come to see that offering kids an authentic alternative to text makes my room more inclusive, and the same tools help all my students show me more of what they know. Different tools enable students to show me how they learn, and paying attention to what they are showing me makes me a more effective teacher.

I was a third-grade classroom teacher for eight years, and recently I became the enrichment teacher in my school. Working with students at many grade levels has confirmed my feeling that well-designed visual tools can engage struggling students and offer exciting challenges to all learners. Working with teachers to help them integrate visual tools, especially storyboard drawing, into their classrooms has given me an opportunity to test strategies in diverse classrooms and at many grade levels. The flexibility of storyboard formats means the tools you use with first graders are easily adapted to serve your advanced fifth graders as well.

Offering my students storyboards and drawing as a thinking tool is the essence of practical differentiated instruction; with any lesson, all my students can use their natural learning skills to get the job done. That's exciting, and it is easy once we try to make our classrooms truly visual. Making a visual classroom is not hard; it is really an attitude that says that any time I can add a visual component to a lesson, I am making my classroom more accessible; I am reaching more learners.

My goal for this chapter is to help you see how easy it can be to use drawing and storyboards to create a visual classroom. I describe how I start the year and make the visual tools a part of learning for my students in all areas of the curriculum throughout the year. I also offer many practical tools and examples of students' work that show how these tools have helped kids succeed.

When I have the opportunity to show my students' work at conferences, teachers quickly recognize how these practical tools make teaching many literacy tasks easier. They tell me, "I know these tools could help my kids, too." That's the exciting part of sharing what I've learned about drawing and visual tools—your students will teach you how to use them because these tools call on kids' natural learning strengths.

BUILDING A CLASSROOM COMMUNITY WITH VISUAL TOOLS

The first few days of the school year are devoted primarily to building a new community with your class and setting ground rules for the rest of the year.

During this time I introduce a valuable visual communication between home and school by using what I call "Weekly News." This is a storyboard that helps kids review their week, and it also serves to inform parents about what's happening in the classroom.

As you can see, it uses a friendly-letter format. The sheet has a box representing each part of the curriculum. I start off every Friday morning going over the week with my class. As a group, we go subject by subject, and I select volunteers to tell about what we did. This is a great way to wrap up each week with your students and get some honest feedback about the events of the week.

Using key words from the students' responses, I draw simple pictures on the board to help the kids with ideas as they set to work on their "News." This may seem like a small change from a written letter to a letter with pictures, but it is so much more. This form of communication truly includes kids with low literacy skills. They can do this work independently. The child reconnects with the knowledge from the week's lessons, and "Weekly News" becomes a personal communication with his or her family.

This weekly news send-home letter helps all students communicate about their week with their families.

STORYBOARDING IN A READING PROGRAM

In this section, I take you through how I start my reading program and introduce storyboarding into my classroom. These techniques can easily be adapted to any grade level. At all grades I strongly recommend a progression of activities that slowly become more complex as students feel more comfortable with storyboarding.

I start my reading program with pattern books as a review of reading comprehension strategies and as a way to connect reading and writing. Books that have a "domino" pattern, such as *If You Give a Mouse a Cookie* by Laura Numeroff, a "repeat word" pattern such as *The Napping House* by Audrey Wood, or a rhyming story such as *Goodnight Moon* by Margaret Wise Brown are all good places to start. Though these books may seem simplistic for third graders, this activity should not be one in which the kids struggle to read words. This activity is designed to strengthen students' ability to recognize patterns, develop prediction skills, and remember sequences, and it shows them they can use techniques they see in reading to write stories of their own.

Thinking about this lesson made me realize how difficult we make activities for many students—especially visual learners. We read a book to them and expect them, page by page, to remember what has happened after we close the book. This is extremely difficult for learners who depend upon visual cues. Beyond picture books, we ask kids to remember what happened in books that we read aloud *without* pictures. Thank goodness there is usually at least one student who has an incredible auditory memory for stories, who can get us all on track. I know that there have been times when I am really not sure where we left off, and my auditory learner savior can tell me faster than I can backtrack in the book.

Storyboarding enables all learners to be successful. It is very effective at this time to talk to the kids about how "real" authors start with storyboards so they can see their ideas all at once. Kids are always surprised to see the simplicity of this strategy that *real* authors use.

First, I read a pattern book and ask the kids if they can determine the pattern. I always start with an obvious pattern, such as rhyming, so they get the concept of a pattern book without a struggle. We then talk about how some patterns are more difficult to figure out. We discuss how you sometimes have to flip the pages back and forth to figure out the pattern. Can they think of a better way? If necessary, explain that the storyboard is the tool we'll use to see the pattern all at once!

This will be the first time we use storyboards in the classroom, so I go over some of the basic rules. Since I will do the initial drawing, we talk about how the pictures will be simple, and that we will use only one to three words in each box, without being concerned with spelling.

When I begin modeling with one of my time-tested favorites, such as *If You Give a Mouse a Cookie*, I draw the main character(s) first—in this case, the insatiable mouse. We start off by agreeing that my mouse drawing, though simple, clearly represents a mouse and that we should draw him the same way each time. We then go through each page and decide what we need to draw to keep things simple but to make sure the pattern will be evident. The first box needs to include the mouse with a cookie. The next box will show the mouse with some milk. Notice

Students can see patterns in the whole story using a storyboard format.

that the drawings are very simple. Some students who like to draw will be tempted to spend more time on each drawing. You need to emphasize that their drawings are a draft and need to be simple—hence, quicker to do or redo, if necessary, during this early stage. They will be able to spend more time later on their final illustrations.

The other important component is the text that will go along with the pictures. We need to keep this simple, too. The first box will say, "Give mouse cookie." The next box will say, "He wants milk." I make sure that it is clear that this is only a draft of our work. We do not have to worry about whether our sentences are complete or whether our spelling is correct. This brings great relief to all students. For those who have difficulty with spelling or aren't sure what a complete sentence is, the pressure is off.

When using storyboarding with pattern books, you need a storyboard square for each page of the book to effectively show the pattern. With books that are longer and more complex, you can use the storyboard to help your students summarize the story by using only one square for each important part. Everything else will be filled in during the retelling. I'll address this in more depth in the read-aloud section.

Once we have completed the storyboard as a whole class, it is time to discuss the pattern. I model how to retell the story in your own words by going through each box of the storyboard and using the pictures and key words. This is another valuable skill for the kids. Once I have retold the story using the storyboard, I ask for volunteers to retell it. How often have you asked a child to use his or her own words to tell you about a story and then cringed as the student struggled to do so? Or he or she is eager to retell the story but ends up having difficulty keeping the sequence straight? By giving kids helpful visual cues, storyboards make so many kids more confident of their abilities. Students who would have never volunteered to retell a story in class will volunteer if they are using a storyboard as a prompt.

Once we have retold the story and the kids can "see" the whole story at one time, more of them will be able to recognize the pattern, that each event causes the next—what we call the "domino" pattern.

Now it is time for the kids to work with a partner to create a storyboard—in this case, a retellingboard, for a different pattern book. Together they must decide how to draw characters and which character is the most important to show. They also select the one to three key words to be in each square. Once the partners are done, they share their work with the class. They retell the story using the retellingboard, and we use their storyboard version of the book to determine its pattern.

EVERYONE CAN BE AN ARTIST

Initially, many children are anxious about drawing, especially in front of their peers. Many teachers are also anxious about drawing in their classrooms. I suffered from that affliction when I started storyboarding with my students. I got over it by telling the kids that they were not allowed to laugh at my pictures just as they would not like me to laugh at theirs. This, of course, makes many of them giggle at whatever I draw. Then there are the "concerned" ones who assure me what a good job I've done no matter what the picture looks like.

THE READING/WRITING CONNECTION

We have now laid a solid foundation for the students to begin to use storyboarding to write their own pattern stories. Working with a partner, the kids choose a pattern book as a model to create their own story.

Once again, it is very important to point out that this is a *draft* of their pattern book. As the partners work on their pattern story, they can easily move around the order of their squares by cutting them out and pasting them on a blank storyboard sheet. When you storyboard, most problems with sequencing or story length are taken care of *before the writing happens*. It is like designing a "no-fault" prewriting tool.

PEER CONFERENCING

Peer conferencing with storyboards is easy. Storyboards allow everyone to literally see the story while the writer is telling it. Writing with storyboards becomes Shared Writing before the work is complete because your students get useful feedback without having to wait for the teacher.

To help your students provide useful feedback, model the process using one of your students' storyboards. Be sure to pick a student who can handle being a guinea pig. When the student is up in the front of the room, ready to retell his or her pattern story, be sure to emphasize that during peer conferences, the goal is for the listener (in this case, the whole class) to help the writer make the story *even better* by asking questions if anything is unclear.

Have the student retell the story from the retellingboard, pointing at each picture as he or she goes. (Be sure to have the class give some positive feedback before the questioning begins.) Ask your students if there is any part of the story where they were unsure of the pattern. Help the student resolve any of these issues so the whole class can see how easy it is to change a retellingboard, especially how little *writing* needs to change. Then ask the class about the order of the story; is there anything that needs to change? Again, work with the student to make any changes in front of the class. Take out the scissors and tape and show how they can change the order without much rewriting or redrawing. This modeling of conferencing may take an entire class session but it will have lasting effects throughout the school year.

This collaboration really makes a difference in the quality of students' work. As students practice peer conferencing, you'll find that by the time students have conferenced with peers and with you, and they feel the story is ready to be written, they know their stories so well that the writing part is much easier. The hard work of revision is done. They can write each page of the story and work on the final illustrations with confidence.

DEVELOPING SUMMARIZING SKILLS WITH STORYBOARDS

Once students have finished storyboarding simple pattern stories, they are ready to use storyboarding to help them remember and retell more complex stories. I use *The Big Orange Splot* by Daniel Pinkwater to start my reading for the year. This is a fun story for the kids, with relatively simple sequencing, and it is also great for introducing the concept of "main idea."

I use Pinkwater's book to work with students on producing a retellingboard that shows only important events, rather than lots of details. (We do not use a storyboard square for every page as we did with the pattern books.) This is a great step toward being able to summarize a story. To help you understand why this story works so well, let's look at the important events:

- Mr. Plumbean, the main character, lives on a neat street where all the houses are the same.
- One day, a bird drops a bucket of paint on his house, causing an orange splot.
- Mr. P.'s neighbors want him to repaint it.
- He repaints it, but paints it to show his dreams.
- His neighbors go to him one by one to try to talk him into changing his house back.
- Instead, they end up changing their own houses to show their dreams.

I begin by reading this story with my students through Shared Reading in small reading groups. We discuss the story as each child reads. Once we have read the story, I tell the students that we will storyboard the important parts together. It never fails that I have students who feel that the most important event to start with is the bird dropping the bucket. This is the fun part for them so they assume it is first. I then ask them why the bird dropping the bucket and causing the splot is important. That helps them realize that we need to start with the fact that the houses are all the same.

In the book, the author shows each of the neighbors going to Mr. P.'s house to talk to him

Retellingboards help students with summarizing and identifying the main idea of the story.

about repainting his house. It is the students' natural tendency to want to do the same with the storyboard and use a square on the storyboard for each neighbor. Instead, we talk about ways to show many neighbors going without having to show each one (see retelling board boxes 9, 10, and 11, page 61). I talk to them about how they are summarizing the important parts of a story when they draw a storyboard: When you retell the story, what you have drawn helps you remember the important parts, and you can fill in the details as you retell.

Once we are done with our class retellingboard, I ask for volunteers to retell the story. It always amazes me that I usually end up with just about every student retelling it. As each student comes up, another feels confident to try. Since we all see and hear the story and build it ourselves, my students end up knowing it by heart! Can you imagine how easy it is for them to answer comprehension questions? All the children in my class know this book: the ones who struggle with reading, the ones who struggle with writing, the ones who struggle with math, and the ones who struggle with little.

STORYBOARDS DURING READ-ALOUD TIME— SHARED READING

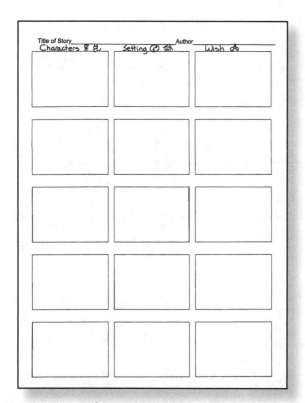

For read-aloud /Shared Reading I use a large storyboard drawn on chart paper.

Storyboards can be adapted to serve almost any curricular purpose. It takes about 20 minutes, a ruler, pencil, and piece of paper to create a storyboard adaptation. When I make a storyboard for Shared Reading, I make it large and laminate it so it is reusable using erasable markers. I create boxes specifically for story elements I feel will be helpful, such as characters, setting, and the main character's wish, as shown here. The rest of the storyboard has boxes for the events of the story.

At the end of each Shared Reading session, I leave an extra 5 to 10 minutes to discuss what we should draw to show the important parts of the story. This discussion helps deepen the students' understanding and clarify their memory of what was just read. I do the drawing for the first read-aloud book. Once the kids feel more comfortable with storyboarding, I ask for volunteers to come up and draw the daily installment. This is not intimidating for them because we determine together how each character should be drawn. The volunteer need only produce what we have decided upon.

You can see here, on our retellingboard of *The Wish Giver* by Bill Brittain, that the characters are drawn very simply, yet each has a specific distinction to help us easily determine who is who. You can see that Thadeus Blinn has a round body, hat, and moustache and that Polly has pigtails. This character distinction also helps you discuss the author's description of characters and character traits.

At the beginning of each Shared Reading, we quickly review what happened during the previous session by retelling the last entries on the storyboard. I have seen participation increase in all discussions about the books since my students have the retellingboard to refer to.

A chapter book takes a long time to finish and is typically harder to summarize than a story you can read in one sitting. Referring to a retellingboard enables students to summarize

All students were able to retell this story using this retelling board.

with ease. By the time I have finished my first long Shared Reading, my students have had quite a bit of experience retelling these stories, so getting a volunteer is not difficult. As with other areas of retelling (pattern books, early books such as *The Big Orange Splot*), once one student breaks the ice, others decide they too can give it a try.

STORYBOARD BOOK PROJECTS

My students became quite comfortable using storyboards once they had the experience of using them with pattern books, their own stories, and read-aloud books. I decided to offer a storyboard as an option for their monthly book projects.

The book projects involved students' independently reading a book at their reading level. Once they finished the book, they were required to do a project that they would present to the class to show that they knew their book well. Traditional project options include dioramas, picture book versions of a book, posters, or games based on the book.

I have found that projects such as dioramas, which show only one key part of the book, do not help the student present the whole story. They also make it difficult to assess how well the student comprehended the whole book. When I added a storyboard version of their book as an option for the book project, many of my students took me up on it. The storyboard they

used was an 11-by-17-inch sheet that was familiar to them from other reading projects. Though our everyday storyboards were simple pictures, I suggested that these could be more detailed and that they could add color. I also suggested that students use a draft storyboard to take notes as they read, no matter what project they chose.

The storyboarding option helped students make presentations that were easy and effective. Since they were used to retelling from storyboards, their presentations were a "piece of cake." It was also easy for me to assess their knowledge of the story. Often during previous book presentations, I had to listen so carefully to follow along that I couldn't enjoy the presentation.

STATE TESTING—HOW STORYBOARDING HELPS

At a conference where Roger and I presented storyboarding to educators from New Hampshire, two third-grade teachers introduced themselves to me. They were excited about the idea of helping their students by incorporating storyboarding but wanted to know what I had done to use it to increase my students' scores on the New Hampshire Educational Improvement and Assessment Program (NHEIAP) test (a standardized state exam administered in third, sixth, and tenth grades). We all know logically that though the test may be given at a particular grade level, it is really testing the child's education thus far. Now those of us unfortunate enough to administer the testing feel personally responsible!

The question posed by these two third-grade teachers hit home with me and made me focus on ways storyboarding could help my students. I had a challenge, and I took it very seriously. My school recently had a workshop on defining areas of weakness on the writing portion of the test. It was very clear that at our school, and most others across the state, "supporting details" were the weakest component of students' writing.

I believe part of the reason for this weakness is that at lower grade levels we tend to concentrate on "story writing." Most of us do not spend as much time on expository writing, teaching students how to express ideas and how to support them. The NHEIAP most often uses prompts that require students to express their ideas, prompts such as these:

- What is your favorite activity? Describe it and give reasons why you like it.
- Who is your favorite person? Tell about them and why you admire them.
- Tell about a famous person. Tell about a day in your life, as if you were that person.

Preparing for the Test

Can you guess what I worked on with my students shortly after the conference?

I began to use—and continue to use—storyboarding to build my students' ability to support their ideas. First, I introduce the writing prompt that is the most concrete and elicits the most ideas from students: the "favorite activity" prompt. Then I give them a series of thinking and drawing prompts to help them brainstorm:

- Draw a picture in the first storyboard box showing you doing the activity.
- Think about all the different times you've done the activity.
- Draw a picture that shows why each time was special.
- Think about with whom you have done the activity.
- Draw a picture of times when you've done this activity with a special person.
- Think about special skills that you have that help you enjoy this activity even more.
- Draw a picture showing you using these skills.

Each box should have one to three key words to help express why each is important. Examples of these key words might be, "With my family," "With best friend," "Won 1st place," "On summer vacation." This will help them when it comes time to write. I then give them a general challenge that I bet they can fill up their whole storyboard with reasons why they enjoy their activity.

As they work, I walk around and give prompts to help them if they're a little stuck. They are really the same prompts that I have already given, only personalized to their particular activity. Once they are finished, I ask them to look over their storyboards and decide what the best thing is about the activity they have drawn. They should put a number 1 in that box. What is the next best? Number that "2." This is a great way for them to review their work in a focused way and to organize their thoughts before they write. (We all know what happens in most cases if we ask the kids to "look over" their work. That is just what they do, they look "over" it, not "at" it.) By giving them a specific task, they are more apt to really think about what they will be writing.

When it is time for them to begin writing, I ask students to think about their first picture (the one of themselves doing the activity). They should use this picture to get started, telling what their favorite activity is and describing it. I then ask them to read the box they have numbered "1" and tell all the things they like about it.

Storyboards increase students' ability to have supporting details in their writing.

Results!

All of my students have produced more writing for this lesson than when they attempted to write without the drawing prompts. The visuals help them express their ideas and hold onto them while they write. This prewriting work prevents the usual writing-avoidance antics, such as kids handing you a half-hearted essay with the proverbial "I'm done," which really means they're tired of writing, so they have ended it prematurely. I've found that students keep going much longer because they have their visuals to guide them and to keep them going. They are not done until they have written about each storyboard box (notice how this student has checked off each square in her camping storyboard as she compared her draft with the original plan).

STORYBOARDING ACROSS THE CURRICULUM

As I became more comfortable with storyboarding during reading and writing, I began to think of other areas in which this visual tool would be helpful. In this next section, we'll look at ways to incorporate these powerful visual tools to support learning across the curriculum.

Social Studies

Since sequencing is an important aspect of storyboards, I decided to use storyboarding during social studies for a time-line activity. Early in the school year we study the Mayflower Pilgrims. Previously, as part of our assignments, I had the kids write down what happened on key dates as we read a book recounting the history of the time period. Though the kids learned about what happened and wrote a sentence next to a date on the worksheet, I can't delude myself into thinking that these dates stuck with most of them.

I knew from my previous experience with visual projects that a visual component would help my students remember and learn about the time period. I had my students draw a picture to go with each date on the Mayflower worksheet. Then they pasted the pictures storyboard fashion on a paper, with their sentence underneath each picture.

It wasn't until later in the school year that I found out just how much more effective this method was for the kids. During a discussion about inventions, the year 1608 came up for a particular invention. From one side of the room, a student said, "1608—I remember that date!" Before he could finish, another student called out, "Yeah, that's when the Pilgrims went to Holland." Others chimed in to confirm that the second student was correct.

An innovative fifth-grade teacher at our school had been using visual tools to teach history for a few years. The fifth-grade curriculum in social studies is American History. That's a lot of information for a fifth grader to grasp in a year. This teacher uses a form of storyboarding to help her kids understand the events leading up to the Revolution (see below). She has found that this visual representation helps her students remember this vast amount of information when she assesses them at the end of the unit. How many students do you think would enjoy reading a history book and then answering questions on a written test rather than drawing a series of pictures to represent the important events?

In both my class and this fifth-grade class, visual methods help students enjoy learning historical facts. It gives kids who struggle with reading and writing a chance to show what they know without having to freeze up because they are faced with pages full of reading or to panic because they have to write sentences.

Storyboards help make learning about history more enjoyable and accessible.

Drawing their visions of these events helped students remember more details about them.

Science

Storyboards have also proven a useful tool in science. I have used them for a few years now as an alternative assessment for our unit on the water cycle. Many students who would struggle with writing down the process can explain it using a water-cycle storyboard. Even those students who have no problem writing it down enjoy the chance to be creative in their drawing of the cycle instead of just recording answers to a test (see the example below).

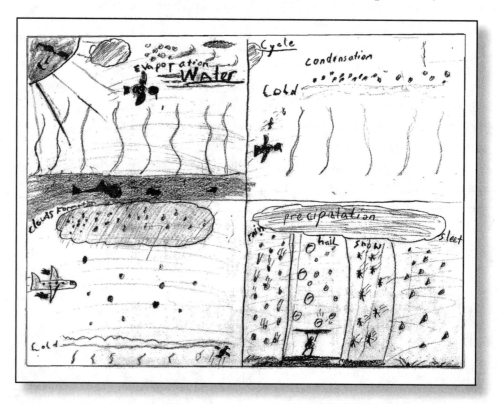

Storyboards are valuable as an alternative assessment tool across the curriculum.

Grammar

I have been having trouble finding a way to teach the concept of nouns and verbs to my students so that they really understand it. I have been experimenting with using a linear storyboard so that they can see the difference between the two parts of speech and how to use them as the building blocks of a descriptive sentence. In the example shown on the next page, I begin with a picture of a noun (*boy*) in the first box. Then I show the noun doing the action/verb (*ran*) in the next box. I also introduce verb expanders (prepositional phrases) that describe how, where, when, and why. In the third box, I add, "The boy ran quickly," and I add lines behind the boy running to show speed. The next box is, "The boy ran quickly down the street," and I add a horizontal line to indicate the street. The fifth box reads, "The boy ran quickly down the street at night," and I show the time of day with a starry sky in the background. The last box adds why the boy ran: "The boy ran down the street at night because he was chased by a dog." And I add the visual to show it.

Using this format shows my students how these parts of speech work within a sentence. It also shows them that building on a sentence, in this case by adding verb expanders, gives their readers a better picture of what they are writing.

This idea can be adapted easily to other grammar topics as well. See what works for your students and the concepts they must learn. If we can reach more students by using visual methods of instruction, we spend less time going back to reteach students who didn't get it.

ANOTHER CLASSROOM SUCCESS STORY

Using drawing helps students understand how adding more description to a sentence enhances the picture that their reader sees.

This year I have a student who is struggling severely with literacy. She has already been retained once so she could have a chance to "catch up." Jenny is in third grade and still reading at a first-grade level.

The first writing task we give our students is a beginning-of-the-year writing sample. We are instructed to give the kids a prompt and to ask them to show us their best writing skills as a beginning third grader. We are not supposed to assist them with this writing. This year, for the first time, we have added a page for the kids to draw a picture to go with their piece, which they may choose to do before or after they write. Most students choose to draw their pictures first.

But even drawing a picture for support was not going to save Jenny from reentering the scary literacy world from which she had escaped during the ten weeks of summer. She quickly reverted to avoidance tactics and struggled excruciatingly to write about a "summer memory." She got through it and wrote a small paragraph about going to the zoo. Jenny also has a lot of difficulty with spelling, so her writing is hard to read. But she got it done. For Jenny, "getting it done" is a big accomplishment.

I introduced my class to storyboarding as a writing tool early in the year when the students worked with partners to write a pattern story. The first time we used it individually was to write family stories. These stories were supposed to have been told to the kids by parents, aunts, uncles, grandparents, or family friends. The kids would then retell the story at school and make a storyboard about it. Jenny chose a story about when her family got a kitten. I do not know whether Jenny really heard this story at home or just decided to write about her experience of getting the kitten. I believe the latter was true because her story started, "My brother, my grandmother, and me were sitting on the sofa. We heard the door. It was Mom and Dad, and they had a kitten." Despite a lot of initial resistance from Jenny, we encouraged her to add to her story and even to make up an exciting part about the kitten being rescued from the river behind her house.

Because it is almost impossible for her to remember the story and to write and spell the required words, Jenny would not have been able to go right into writing this story. However, Jenny was comfortable with drawing and was, therefore, able to storyboard the story. Once her retellingboard was finished and she had told her story to teachers and classmates, she knew it well enough to write it. The writing was still a struggle for her (imagine what it is like to have such difficulties with spelling that you can't even reread your own writing!)—and she resisted some, but not as much. Knowing the story so well helped her to write the story and do more spelling editing than I'd ever seen her do.

The true success of this storyboarding experience did not reveal itself until later. The students were choosing writing pieces for their portfolio and Jenny chose her kitten story. She came up to me with the cover sheet she used to write about why she chose the piece and was beaming as she proudly exclaimed that this was the longest piece she had ever written. I think that for Jenny, "proud" and "writing" had never been associated.

YOU DON'T NEED A MAGIC WAND

Even though Roger referred to me as the Fairy Godmother earlier in this book, I hope that I have shown you that the last thing you need is a magic wand. The only magic I possess has been given to me by the children I teach. They have shown me how drawing and telling make learning easier. Watching them draw, listening to them build ideas, watching them struggle less, and trying to see things through their eyes has convinced me I must offer them tools they can use. The visual tools that I have created took basic classroom supplies and a little bit of time to make. And every time I use these tools, it becomes a more natural way to teach. I revise as I go. Every time I draw with my students and listen to their ideas I see how these different tools help us all learn from each other. Your students are eager to teach you. Please give it a try.

Chapter 6

Reading Comprehension: Core Visual Skills

We've seen how storyboards support writers and readers in both Amy Rocci's and Linda Rief's classrooms. Here I want to focus on Shared Reading, a process where storyboards and drawing are used to support class reading and discussion.

Let's begin by studying what can block struggling readers. Then we'll see how drawing pictures can break those blocks. We'll also take a quick look at comprehension research that shows why storyboarding/drawing is uniquely suited to teaching comprehension skills. Then we'll see how a visual reading process, linked to Readers Theater for older students, boosts engagement and comprehension.

READING BLIND

My first practical demonstration of the power of drawing as a reading comprehension tool came when my son Andy brought home his first chapter book in fourth grade. Andy was excited. As he handed me a biography of Louis Braille, he flipped proudly through the pages to show me there were no pictures. Getting your first chapter book in school is a rite of passage, a statement of accomplishment. Andy understood his teacher was telling him, "You are growing up, becoming a real reader. You are ready to read independently, and you don't need those baby pictures anymore."

I remember the special allure of chapter books: all those pages in adult code—stories and secrets only grown-up readers can share. Text-only, that's what the smart kids read. By fourth grade, my twin sister had been reading chapter books forever, sailing through Nancy Drew books like she was watching a great TV serial. The first chapter book I read completely was in

the eighth grade, and it wasn't fun. I was sent to my room for the weekend: "Read until you finish." Fortunately, it was a good story about Indians and bloody torture. When I reached the last page it was Sunday, and the winter sun was just going down. I emerged, glad I was done, and convinced that I would never read easily or for pleasure. I didn't want Andy to learn what I learned. For me, the promise of chapter books was confirmation I was not smart enough.

For Andy, reading was already too hard, and his class was leaving the picture books we both loved behind. Everyone was doing independent and small-group reading. Eager to fit in, Andy participated. He could decode sentences well enough to appear to be keeping up; he read along without protest or saying, "I don't get this." But we knew if you scratched below his eager-to-please façade, you'd find he was faking it, missing too much. Tests confirmed his comprehension was "significantly below grade level."

ONE-ON-ONE FAILURE

I scanned his book, flipping through pages of dense text. Then, trying to sound upbeat, I suggested we read together, "just to get you started." After several protests from Andy that he was supposed to do this by himself, we sat with the book between us. He read a page to me, pointing to the words, his reading slow but clear. Then I read a page to him, having him continue to point so I could tell he was focusing. He considered my reading out loud "cheating," but it was clear he was overwhelmed by trying to decode new words and follow the story at the same time. As we read about Louis Braille's early life in a strange time and a country, I saw Andy pushing relentlessly forward. When I suggested we pause to explain old-fashioned words or to talk about history he didn't know, he became frustrated. It seemed the goal of "independent reading" was simply *consuming text*.

Note the bind I was in as a parent. Andy saw help as undermining his "independent reading assignment." Yet it was immediately clear no one had made a thoughtful choice of a text he might grasp. If Andy had been offered a text with lots of pictures, views of horse-and-buggy Paris, for instance, it could have made his reading more engaging and meaningful.

Unfortunately the curriculum goal is learning through pure text. Remember that famous saying: "In third grade *we learn to read*; in fourth grade *we read to learn*." Andy's classroom was following that logic in the common push to chapter books designed to help kids focus on text alone. I've heard this strategy recommended as "weaning": helping kids discard "visual crutches" like picture books. Weaning is common practice, with costly unintended side effects. Weaning also creates a memorable

image—yanking those visual crutches away from struggling learners. Andy's quiet reading failure is a typical example of the no-win bind "weaning" creates for teachers, intentionally withdrawing visual supports, yet not being able to provide one-on-one help for all the stragglers.

READING HELP?

Andy and I read together that Louis was born with normal sight. He was playing with his father's leather-working tools and accidentally stabbed himself in the eye. His other eye became infected, and Louis became blind. I stopped wincing. Andy seemed unmoved, ready to push on to the next chapter. I asked what he knew about blindness. When Andy said, "I'm not sure," I realized he had no idea what Louis faced. Andy had no idea what *blind* meant. That's when I knew for sure we had to slow down.

We talked, then tried blindfolding our eyes, and soon we were stumbling into furniture. At bedtime Andy was still processing. Before I turned the light off Andy said, with some urgency, "Dad, I don't want to be blind." As I went downstairs, I thought I'd done a good job as his reading teacher.

The next night after dinner Andy got his book. Before we started Chapter 2 I asked, "Let's review—what happened in the story last night?" Andy looked at me puzzled. It was a long minute before he said, "I can't remember, Dad." Several tries at getting even the basics of the story from him led me to, "If you would only pay attention. . . ." You'd think as a failed reader I'd be sympathetic. But no, I was getting a big dose of what it was like teaching Andy. My focused help was making reading more painful.

As Andy's "teacher," I was lost. I'd tried all the things I knew about helping weak readers: reading aloud and discussing the story. We'd even acted out the main character's problem—I had a bruise on my shin from the coffee table to prove it.

Please note that when I read with Andy, I used reading aloud with focused discussion to help overcome his weak reading skills. These may be the two most widely used strategies designed to help struggling readers. Teachers, lacking the time for one-on-one intervention, use read-alouds with classroom discussion, hoping to include everyone in a fluid reading experience. Reading groups and Readers Theater are popular outgrowths of this idea. Unfortunately, Andy had shown me that, for him, reading aloud with discussion didn't help much.

Completely stuck, I had a flash of insight that scared me. What if Andy really couldn't remember most of what we read? For me, that image of Louis poking his eye with an awl was unforgettable. But Andy couldn't seem to remember it without a lot of prompting. That night I was struck by how deep Andy's reading problems seemed to be. If Andy couldn't remember what he read, then how was he going to survive in school?

VISUALIZATION RESEARCH

Only later, after reading research on comprehension, did I learn Andy's reading problems were dramatic and all too common. The transition from *learning to read* to *learning comfortably from reading* can be daunting and mysterious. Comprehension is a complex process many students struggle with long past fourth grade. In fact, research shows weak reading comprehension is a critical problem for many older readers. The good news is researchers are in remarkable agreement about what does help, about what underpins and supports comprehension: visualization.

Ellen Keene, in *Mosaic of Thought*, makes a convincing case, reinforced many times, that engaged and effective reading is, at heart, visualization,

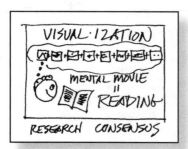

or creating and capturing mental images as we read. And Keene also shows with classroom detail how our conventional reading/discussion strategies fail to teach essential visualization skills students need (1997).

Nanci Bell, a well-known reading/speech specialist, summarizes succinctly the research consensus about the role of visualization in reading by saying effective readers "make a mental movie as they read" (1991, p. 3). We are about to see a practical demonstration of the way drawing can make mental visualization into a hands-on memorable experience for a young reader.

A FIRST READER'S STORYBOARD

Recognizing I'd failed Andy with conventional reading strategies, I decided to try something different; we would storyboard Andy's book as we read—

Andy's first try at a three-square summary of the first chapter of the Braille biography

much the same as Amy Rocci's students had done with *Cinderella*. I had no idea if it would help, or if Andy would try it, since he was already fed up with my help.

I got a large sheet of drawing paper and drew three simple boxes across a blank sheet. With some coaching, we reconstructed the opening events in the first chapter of the story.

Andy decided to start with a drawing of Louis. In the first box, he drew Louis Braille with good eyes; in the second, Louis playing with pointed tools; in the third, Louis with a tool sticking in his eye, resulting in his blindness (the fourth box).

Andy and I read the next chapter. Then we discussed what three images Andy might draw to summarize the chapter. Andy drew Louis going to the well to get water because the story said that despite his blindness, Louis's parents made him do chores like the other kids. The next picture showed how Louis got around without sight—he used his ears.

Each night, before we read the next chapter, Andy would retell me the story from his storyboard as a review. He did not read the squares as a fixed thing; he simply used each square as cues to remind him of the story. For the first square he might say, "Louis Braille could see fine when he was born. . . ." Within a few nights, Andy was recounting events in the early chapters easily. This repeated picture review was locking the main events of the story in his head. He found this review gave him a clear road map back into the story.

Andy's summary of the first five chapters of the Braille biography

The concrete support this simple board gave Andy was immediately obvious. As we read the book and discussed it, Andy was drawing notes that became a visual outline of the story. Unlike a text-only outline, this picture-rich sequence, all on one page, made it possible for him to easily see particular events step by step, and also see an overview of the whole book and the flow of the story.

The steps in our process became discussing what was worth recording, drawing, and adding key words to in order to convey the main ideas. Then Andy would retell the story from his pictures. It was easy to see how each step helped him grasp the reading. His picture notes reminded him where he'd been, and as we progressed in the story, he had more context for understanding events. He relaxed and read with more confidence.

Equally important, his storyboard became our *shared map* of the story, one that supported Andy and gave me a powerful window into his comprehension: His decisions about what to draw, what key words to write, and

how he retold the story from his pictures made it easy to know what he got and what he was missing. By the time we'd finished the book, Andy could tell you the whole story, how Louis Braille struggled with his blindness and how he had to struggle to overcome sighted folks' preconceptions about how blind people should learn to read.

SHARED READING: CORE COMPREHENSION

From that first board with Andy came comprehension experiments in many classrooms. Students of all backgrounds and skill levels have continued to confirm what Andy showed us: When readers create concrete pictures to track and review what they read, comprehension soars. The reasons are not mysterious when we consider what researcher Nanci Bell discovered from a student. When she asked how he so easily remembered what he read he said, "I just see movies inside my head when I read. The words turn into pictures, and I just remember the pictures." Bell was struck by this movie analogy, and in time she found that all competent readers use a visualization "movie" to capture a flow of words. As she explored research on learning, from Aristotle to Piaget, Bell came to the conclusion that we read in pictures because *we naturally think in pictures* (1986, p. 7).

Bell's metaphor of reading as mental movie-making is now so widely accepted it can seem obvious. Space does not allow a full exploration of wide-ranging research that supports Bell's larger conclusion that we think in pictures. But let me suggest, if thinking in images seems a strange idea, perhaps common sense may help. Tell me when you last dreamed in text, or even in words alone? Dreaming is the mind on visualization vacation, making mental movies just for fun, until you wake and need your mind's focused visualization skills to capture new events, a new story, or a complex essay.

At the risk of oversimplifying, Bell realized many young readers don't know how to use their visualization skills when reading text. They need help recognizing and capturing the fleeting mental images that come from text. Before they can get meaning from a complex flow of words they must have a way to grab and hold onto the flow.

Andy showed us that drawing can focus a reader's natural visualization skills. When we teach students to capture mental images as they read, we are teaching the basic mechanics of comprehension at its visual core. As students learn how to record their mental images in simple drawings, those images become concrete notes that make any reading memorable.

You can see, in both Amy Rocci's and Linda Rief's classrooms, there are many ways storyboards can support comprehension, from taking notes to learning vocabulary to building and writing a reader's response. Here I want to outline the steps in a Shared Reading process designed to accompany all-class or group reading.

THE SHARED READING PROCESS

Shared Reading uses a large storyboard as a visual focus/support for class reading and discussion. This board can take many forms, but I recommend a retellingboard, a large poster board with moveable cards, similar to the tellingboard we saw writers use earlier. This retellingboard might be thought of as a visual note-taking tool used by the entire class (or a reading group). The design with moveable cards offers both a flexible format and the ability to easily revise content.

Teachers Kara Coggeshall and Jim Doherty use an all-class retellingboard to record events in a novel.

A retellingboard can be set up to support any reading: a textbook, a single current events article, or a whole novel. The process can support a whole class or small reading groups, with each group using their own board. Retellingboards can be adapted to fit many tasks; the number and size of the squares is determined by the grade level and the needs of the class. Three or four squares across generally works well, but the complexity and length of chapters, and the level of detail your students need, should guide how you set up your boards.

In many classrooms, teachers find it helpful to have students write on individual storyboard sheets to accompany the large whole-class storyboard. I try to design the smaller sheet to be identical in pattern to the big board so class notes and individual notes look the same. Students' sheets can be 8½ by 11 inches in older grades, with as many as 24 squares—11 by 17 inches in younger grades.

Shared Reading: Basic Steps

Using a retellingboard to support students' reading is straightforward. The aim is to build a simple map, in pictures and text, as reading

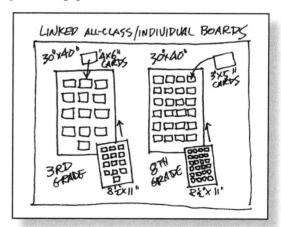

There are many ways to sequence information in a single storyboard square.

proceeds. We make the key events in the story visible so the evolving plot is there for all to see. We can also show character reactions, ideas, and themes the story raises. You will find a well-constructed story map is a strong support for all learners. Students enjoy storyboard review, and it is a great focusing tool.

The large retellingboard will be the focus of class reading and discussion. In addition, allowing each student to use his or her own storyboard sheet to parallel the progress on the big board invites full participation and makes the hands-on process memorable. Here are the basic steps used with a class reading a novel over an extended period, using both a large-group retellingboard and individual boards.

1. Read Reading can be done silently or aloud, with you or your students reading and everyone else following the text in the book. At the end of a passage of suitable length, one that all students can remember easily, begin the class discussion. (See also Storyboards With Readers Theater on pages 83–85.)

2. Discuss/Draw Ask students to summarize what they have just read. You might say, "Everyone, tell me in four squares what you think are the most important events in this chapter." You're asking for notes on main points using simple drawing and a few key words like headlines; you want this to be focused and simple, no fancy drawing or full sentences. A teacher might add, "Give me those four squares in four minutes."

3. Share Notes Once students complete their squares, the whole class can literally compare notes, share, and discuss what images/ideas best summarize the reading.

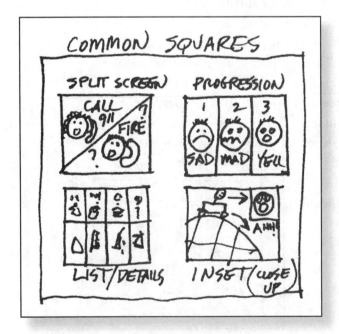

There are many ways to sequence information in a single storyboard square.

More than just a great way to review story content, this visual verbal sharing helps readers build key comprehension skills. The sequenced storyboard images illustrate the essential mechanics of hidden mental visualization skills—letting everyone see and discuss the mental-movie-making process. By linking students' natural drawing and talking skills with reading visualization skills we support all learners.

4. Create Cards Once the class agrees on the ideas needed on cards, have several students create cards for the big board (or create the cards yourself). Because these cards will be "read" by all learners, they need to be clear and well-planned. A single square can contain several events or ideas but they need to be simple, bold-

face, headline-style text, so folks in the back row can see them. Squares can be subdivided in a "split screen" or divided into parts to emphasize steps or details. (See below for more on readability.)

5. Retelling/Revising Once the passage is on the board in a sequence of cards, a verbal retelling is the best way to be sure the notes are easy to read and effective. Have a student come up and retell from the board. This is a good review of the class discussion, but it is also a great opportunity to see what students have understood. If a student's retelling is rough, if the teller stumbles on a square, or if key ideas get left out of the telling, then that is a signal that the notes need revision. We need to add to the storyboard or change a square. Discuss and revise the pictures or key words until retelling is easy.

6. Review Before Next Reading For any extended reading, over several days or weeks, when a new session of reading begins, having students retell from the class storyboard is essential. This retelling is a good review and a way to gauge kids' grasp of the full story. Indeed, asking struggling readers to retell is a great way to be sure the board works and that they are with you. Again, if these kids have trouble retelling, if they get stuck on a square, that square needs to be revised.

MAKING EFFECTIVE INCLUSIVE NOTES

Simple icons can create a potent memory map of the content. We know memory is image-linked, and simple drawings are all the more memorable when students help create the image ideas. Building a community story map can support all learners, especially struggling students. Creating concrete images of the evolving story means everybody—even folks with weak memory, sequencing, or visualization skills—can grasp events and join in the discussion with confidence.

Visual notes, like text notes, need to be built in a clear, logical way. When students retell/review from the class board, the teacher has a great opportunity see how students use visual tools. We can learn with our students how to create clear, easy-to-read notes.

Before a student starts retelling, I make a point of saying, "If you get stuck on a square, it means our notes need to be fixed." Keep in mind that asking your best readers to retell visual notes will only confirm they can bypass obstacles and juggle confusing information. Asking students who struggle with sequencing to retell will give the class notes a better road test. Students who struggle will show you which squares are easy to read and which are "sticky." Students who get stuck will help everyone learn how to make visual notes that are user-friendly.

The elements in each square, pictures and key words, are there to anchor ideas and remind a teller what to say. You will learn from your students what level of detail and what order of placing elements in a square best helps students capture and use information.

If, for example, a student retelling a square leaves out that the dad is bald and that's an important detail, adding the key word *bald* to the square tells everyone that it's worth remembering. In the same way, if the key word doesn't help, if the point of the square is dad is upset, then *bald* may divert the teller. *Bald* can be written small and UPSET big.

Watching kids retell, and revising squares that do not work well for kids, offers a great opportunity to learn how students process visual information. By experimenting with the order of elements within a square and with key words, you can learn how to help all learners be successful. Here are some basic ideas I've seen.

- Squares built to follow "text logic," with events and key words flowing from left to right, top to bottom, are easier to read. For kids with emerging text skills, following text logic reinforces literacy goals, too.

- Breaking complex events into parts is especially helpful for students with sequencing/logic and speech issues.

- Squares might contain an event and a close-up of a character's reaction as well, to help the teller grasp the drama in events.

- Key words that refer to actions and emotions are more effective than object labels. (See more on effective key words in Chapter 7.)

Shared Reading: Inclusive Reading Community

We've seen how effective storyboards can be in reaching kids at the margins of the writing classroom. Now I want to offer a reading story that shows how low-text tools pull everyone into a reading circle. We will see how Shared Reading transformed a remarkably diverse class into a reading community.

Jim Doherty and Kara Coggeshall taught in a small-town middle school, where most of the students are mainstreamed in Language Arts. Yet each year in a seventh-grade class of about 100, approximately ten kids were believed to have learning challenges so severe that they were pulled from the regular classes and sent to the Resource Room, where they worked with

Jim. The kids in his class had a range of issues, from dyslexia to severe hyperactivity, accompanied by poor reading comprehension, which excluded them from the mainstream classroom. Jim gave them lots of support and one-on-one help. He also cotaught in the regular Language Arts classroom with Kara, where other Special Ed kids were mainstreamed.

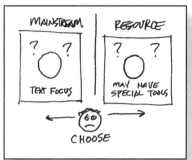

Jim and Kara enjoyed coteaching; it gave them the opportunity to share ideas and experiment with techniques that might include more of the kids. Still, Kara was always uncomfortable with the idea that she rarely saw the Resource Room kids. Jim was also frustrated. He knew these kids got more one-on-one help in the Resource Room, but there was also a stigma attached to getting that special help.

COTEACHING

What to do? Jim had started experimenting with storyboards in the Resource Room and bringing them to the mainstream class when he cotaught with Kara. They had a workshop with Linda Rief, who shared her experience with Readers Theater, which involves kids taking the role of a character in the story, reading prehighlighted parts, and discussing the reading as a group. After experimenting with integrating storyboards into their mainstream curriculum, they decided these tools might make full, meaningful inclusion possible. They decided to try a big experiment.

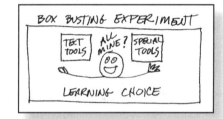

With the support of parents and administration, the teachers temporarily changed placement for Language Arts and brought all those kids into an integrated classroom. The result was a room many teachers might see as a potential disaster. The class consisted of 25 kids with reading levels from third grade to twelfth grade, nearly half of whom had learning disabilities, including significant developmental and emotional issues and disruptive behaviors.

FIRST BOOK: IS *WALK TWO MOONS* TOO HARD?

When Jim shared their inclusion plan with me, he said they were hoping to begin Shared Reading with the book *Walk Two Moons* by Sharon Creech. He loaned me the book to see what I thought. It's a Newbery Medal winner, with an engaging main character, but by the second chapter I had serious reservations about the complex structure of the story. Here's a brief synopsis: A girl on a road trip across Middle America with her grandparents tells the old folks a complex mystery to pass the time. Interconnected flashbacks, interspersed with the events on the road, are woven together, resulting in a climax where all the characters are dramatically and psychologically linked, and the long-held mystery is revealed.

For comfortable readers, sorting out this kind of dense narrative is part of the fun. But these teachers were collecting all the struggling readers they could find. I went to Jim to discuss my concerns. I was pointing out why the complex two-track time structure of the book would be especially tough when I thought of another book I'd storyboarded with Andy, *Timothy of the Cay* by Theodore Taylor. That story had the same split-time structure. When I showed that storyboard to Jim, we both knew right away what the answer was.

A TWO-TRACK STORYBOARD

Timothy of the Cay is a sequel to *The Cay*, a straightforward narrative about a ship that was torpedoed in World War II, and a boy's and an old man's struggle for survival on a small island. The linear plot and limited characters of the first book gave Andy confidence in reading. When he chose the sequel, I assumed it would be easy, too, especially since the main characters would be the same. Think again. He began reading the book and was immediately confused. I sat with him to see what was up.

The story starts as a straight narrative with familiar characters, but in Chapter 2 it goes *pop*! Suddenly the reader is rocketed back 60 years to the childhood of the old man. The book then proceeds on two separate tracks: one story set in the 1940s, the other in the 1890s. For Andy, each chapter meant a massive mental shift: a character who had been an older adult was suddenly a child. He had real trouble making sense of it, keeping track of characters and events, and again discussion wasn't helping much. We went back to the drawing board.

The solution we arrived at—the split-time storyboard shown at right—solved our problem immediately. As we began reading each chapter, Andy had to decide which side of the board we were on. The new ship symbol at the top of the left column and the old sailing ship on the right help make that time shift clear.

Andy drew events on the split board, and the dual time structure of the book became visible. If he needed to explain the book to his class, this storyboard would make a complicated structure simple to show.

All Text Is a Problem

You can see Andy is more comfortable with text on this board than his earlier one. In fact, sometimes his squares are all text. That is often the sign of a problem. I try to encourage students to keep text spare. A board with a lot of text becomes hard to read. I find squares with lots of text often mean the student is not summarizing well, not coming up with strong images in his head. Generally, clear pictures mean the student has a strong grasp of the main points and spare text is enough.

A split storyboard format tracks the main plot alongside the secondary flashback plot.

STORYBOARDS WITH READERS THEATER

Jim and Kara created a focused prereading process for *Walk Two Moons* that helped kids get oriented before they began group reading. Students did online research that included finding visuals of the road trip destinations: Yellowstone, Mount Rushmore, and the Badlands. From that search they predicted what the story would be about.

As the students began Readers Theater with *Walk Two Moons*, they followed the basic steps in the Shared Reading process outlined above and created a few adaptations of their own:

1. The class read the story out loud, with some students taking the various parts highlighted in their books and the rest of the class following the text.

2. After each reading, all students storyboarded the main events on individual storyboards, working fast, as if they were playing a game of Pictionary.

3. Following that came lively discussion of the main points and the images and words that worked best. During discussion students made suggestions about what cards for the all-class board should show. Several students made final cards and added them to the board for the class to road-test with a retelling. Students may choose to revise their individual boards to parallel the content on the all-class board.

A STORYBOARD ASIDE

As Andy and I read *Timothy of the Cay* and I saw the parallel structure, I began to suspect that the author did not write the story in chapter order, but built the two narratives separately and then wove them together. He might have used a board much like the one we created to plan how the two stories would dovetail in the final book. Certainly that's what many authors do when planning a complex structure. I've heard authors say, "I got a big cork board, and I worked on file cards, moving them around." That's a storyboard.

Jim and Kara saw immediately the storyboard process pulled in kids who never really participated in reading before. They found students engaged for many reasons: Some liked to read aloud, others wanted to draw, others wanted a chance to show what they knew by retelling from the big board. And the ones most eager to retell were often kids who had been silent before. With the board as a script for retelling, they could speak with confidence. The shared storyboard focused everyone, so they could participate and succeed.

With concrete visual support for all readers, class discussion became more focused and more productive. The class storyboard created visible scaffolding on which to contemplate the whole story. Best of all, with a common story map available, Jim and Kara found they could raise the bar and have more sophisticated in-depth class discussions. To try to go deeper without a visible outline means we usually leave a lot of kids behind. With storyboards as common class notes, discussing connections or patterns, like the time shifts, is easy because students can refer to the picture map of the story.

A split storyboard of *Walk Two Moons*: The road trip action (present) is pictured on the right while the mystery story action (past) is pictured at left.

Kara said, "We actually pictured three plots on the *Walk Two Moons* board, because Sal has flashbacks of her mother. We denoted a flashback by drawing a squiggly, cloud-like shape around the entire picture so kids knew that scene was happening in the past. It was a student's idea, I believe."

With a full board map, the class can visually track the rising action or explore underlying themes. As Jim put it, "Storyboarding is visual and it involves a second medium that non-included students are usually very comfortable with: speaking. You don't just draw the plot, you talk about it in class. As a result, there was no shortage of involvement and that group excelled."

A cloud shape signals a flashback "third plot" in *Walk Two Moons.*

The retelling board became a focus for discussion, and when it was time to write, it became a support for writing as well. Jim and Kara found students' storyboards served as personal book notes, which helped both reluctant and experienced writers to brainstorm and organize ideas for written responses to their reading.

The teachers might ask, "In your storyboard notes, can you find squares that show the ways the main character grows?" They also created shorter storyboard formats designed to help students organize their writing. Offering students a storyboard with lines below squares for text notes, they might suggest, "Use your boards to show places where the character has had to change." Students spent ten minutes storyboarding their ideas, then the teachers said, "Now, using those events recorded on the storyboard, write a short essay on this character's transformation. Use your storyboard as an outline."

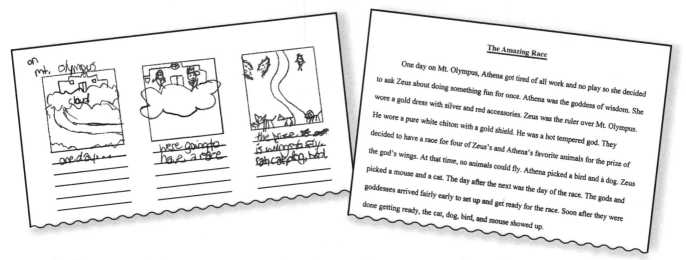

Reading response leads to writing as Doherty's students create an original myth. Here a girl's storyboard notes outline a myth that begins, "One day on Mt. Olympus, Athena got tired of all work and no play. . . ."

INCLUSION AND DIFFERENTIATION, TOO

This inclusion experiment was an unqualified success. These coteachers showed that with solid visual support, all their students could succeed in the mainstream classroom. In Jim's words, "Because it involves familiar skills, the storyboarding was the glue that held inclusion together."

Jim summarized his experience on the way visual support created a reading community: "Storyboarding is differentiated instruction personified. It reaches all learners on so many levels. For kids who are struggling, it makes reading (and writing) accessible in the regular classroom. For the middle levels, it makes the teaching of abstract literary concepts visual. For the most skilled students, it introduces them to a tool that can open up worlds in their reading that take them out of the galaxy. And the amazing thing is, storyboards accomplish all this at the same rate of instruction without kids falling behind or growing bored."

BECOMING VISUAL THINKERS

Shared Reading and Writing are essentially linked. In fact, as Amy Rocci showed us, many teachers find Shared Reading is the ideal way to introduce and hone everyone's storyboard skills before going to storyboards for writing.

Shared Reading tools for group note-taking and review can easily be adapted to many classroom tasks. Having the whole class (or groups) storyboard any reading or lesson, in language arts, science, math, or social studies, is a great review, and it is the essence of inclusion and collaboration. Discussion with pictures, text, and verbal input touches all the learning bases, helping students to learn from one another and to appreciate everyone's strengths and contributions.

You want your students to be strong visual thinkers, and storyboarding with them will hone your own visual thinking skills, too. The teacher who can make dry material interesting with good visuals, a diagram on the board, or with memorable visual language teaches more effectively. Using a storyboard to accompany reading or talk is teaching kids to take memorable notes. Teaching with images develops effective mental processing skills that will serve students well when they are reading a novel or a textbook or summarizing a lecture.

Making a Classroom Retelling Board

You will want to prepare some poster-size boards that you can store easily. For an all-class board I recommend foam core, which is very lightweight. Office supply stores usually carry 20-by-30- or 30-by-40-inch boards, but art supply stores often have additional sizes. With a yardstick and a marker it's easy to mark out a simple grid to fit whatever size index cards you plan to use. You'll want a board big enough so that kids in the last row can read what's on the cards.

The size of the board, and the layout of the storyboard (for example, will it have four squares across or only three) is flexible and determined by the complexity of the task. A big board will accommodate many chapters of a novel; a smaller board may be sufficient for review of a short passage from a science text. If I'm working with younger students, I use a storyboard with discrete squares for large cards to fit in; with older students, a simple grid will do, and the size and density of the cards can increase without overwhelming kids visually.

The cards can be any size that allows everyone to see what's on the board. I generally use standard 3-by-5- or 4-by-6-inch file cards. They are cheap and have enough substance so they can be moved around without tearing or wrinkling. They can also be stored easily.

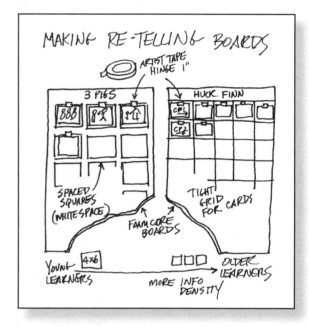

Retelling boards can be designed to fit the needs of younger and older students.

Sticky notes will work, but they send a message that this is just temporary, and they do not transport or stack easily if you intend to keep the results of the class work. For smaller-group sharing—reading groups, for example—smaller cards and boards will do.

I strongly recommend using artist's tape for your storyboards. This looks like white masking tape, and was designed for page layout. It can go on and off many times without tearing the surface of the board.

Chapter 7

Introducing Storyboards and Drawing in the Classroom

Storyboards are hands-on drawing and telling tools, and they are most easily shared in the classroom *live*. I generally introduce the storyboard writing process to students and teachers by drawing and retelling a famous story on a big whiteboard with squares on it.

This second grader is helping me storyboard *The Three Little Pigs.*

With young kids, I might draw as I retell the story of *The Three Little Pigs*. With older students, I use the story of the sinking of the Titanic, telling the story with stick pictures and minimal text while discussing the basic elements of picture-writing on storyboards (see Appendix A, page 125). As students get an overview of storyboards as a writing tool, I'm also showing how the steps in the Shared Writing process parallel the traditional writing process, from brainstorming through several steps of revision.

Visual Outline: From Shared Writing to Making a Picture Book

When I'm starting a writing residency where students will collect a family story and create a picture book, I use the writing process storyboard shown below. This 13-square visual outline is designed to let me give an overview of the steps in the storyboarding/story building/bookmaking process. The power of this tool is clear when you see how both first graders and grad students can follow and remember the steps in the process.

This board shows how picture-book writers will use the same Shared Writing process we saw in Linda Rief's eighth-grade classroom. This board gives everybody an easy overview of the process, but it is also my trusted outline for speaking. This visual outline connects the audience and the speaker in a unique way.

Some of the squares are easy to read/decode. The first square, for example, is clearly about getting a story to tell. Other squares may be harder to read. That's okay. This kind of storyboard is supposed to communicate, but not stand alone. This picture outline is designed to work with an explanation (given aloud) of each square. A well-designed storyboard should remind the speaker what to tell the audience, square by square, and remind the audience what the speaker "said" in each square when he or she is finished.

Flexible Speaking Tool

The way I tell each square from this board depends on my audience. If I'm sharing with second graders, I will try to keep my telling simple, a sentence or two with each square, so everyone can remember what I said with each step. If I'm presenting to older students or to teachers, I can talk a lot more about each step. For square one, for example, I can describe how to elicit a good story and the way a good listener can help draw out more of the story. The storyboard is my loose script/outline for talking about the process.

At the same time, the storyboard serves as my audience's ready-made notes. It allows them to follow along, and to look back or ahead without worrying that they're missing anything. That's the power of the storyboard: it puts us all on the same page.

Shared Writing Summary

The beginning squares of this board introduce the basic steps in the Shared Writing process. Let me *tell* the process as I might to an audience of young students, and I'll add some commentary as we go. As we go forward you will notice we are paralleling the basic steps of the text-writing process. The first two squares are prewriting: brainstorming and thinking about the hook. Square three is drafting, and on to conferencing in square five."

BRAINSTORMING

Square 1 To collect a family story, you need to find someone with a story to tell. Then you need to listen carefully to their story. The pictures and the text reinforce my telling. The big ear reminds us about really listening. The smile says it's a good story.

Square 2 Once we have a story, we think about what the hook is in the story. The hook is the funny/scary/exciting part. The hook is the reason other people want to hear your story. "When my uncle jumped off the roof" is a hook. It gets everybody's attention. We will build our story around the hook.

We share our hook and try to retell the hook in a sentence or two. This is our tryout, our condensed first draft. If we can tell the hook in a few words and make it so compelling that other people show they are interested in hearing more of the story, then we are ready to start storyboarding.

DRAFTING

Square 3 We storyboard our story in as many squares as we think it takes to tell it well. Some stories start with only six squares; others might use all 13. We might even need two sheets if our story is extra long. We put pictures and a few key words in each square, but we keep both simple so our storyboard is easy to read.

CONFERENCING AND REVISION

Square 4 After we have storyboarded our first draft of the story, it's time to share our storyboard. Our stick-pic student has a six-square story. You can see how he tells, pointing to the squares in his story.

Square 5 When we are finished, our audience reacts to our telling. You can see that some folks in the audience may like this telling; others may not. They say, "Huh?" It's the "Huh" folks you want to pay special attention to. The people who have questions about your story are your best story-building helpers.

In this stick-pic figure, next to the audience we see the teller's new storyboard. You can see that it's longer; it's a nine-square story now, because this teller's audience must have had good questions, and they helped the teller add to the story.

You'll notice that square 5 has a lot to tell about. That's because in one square I show the entire conferencing/revision process. If a picture is worth a thousand words, one picture about conferencing and revision is not enough. (In Chapter 8 we will look at the way tellingboards make revision easier and more engaging for students.) Certainly we should highlight this conferencing square and say that this revision step is the key to improved writing, and it is best done several times: tell, revise, tell, revise.

TRANSITION TO TEXT

Square 6 This square says "MAKE BOOK," but it is really the transition to text. Let's imagine we have told and revised our story several times, and our audience now says our story is pretty good. It's time to begin writing text. The transition from storyboard telling to text is straightforward: Students put their verbal telling onto the page in text—a transition that becomes more exciting if we use an actual picture-book format.

Using a sample dummy book, I show how seven sheets of folded printer paper stapled together make a draft book. We actually make a photocopy of

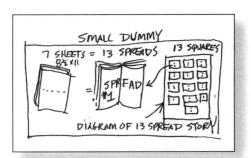

a student's storyboard, saving the original as a first draft of the story. Then we cut up the copy and paste all the squares into the dummy book. Each left-hand page in the book is one square of the storyboard. Text relating to that square will go on a sheet of paper pasted onto the right-hand page.

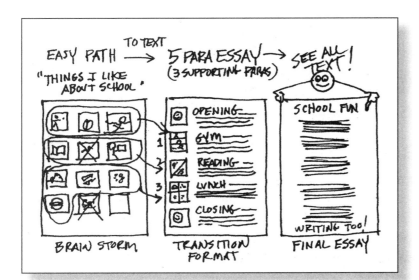

Older students also need a clear transitional format from brainstorming in pictures to text. Here, a storyboard path moves from brainstorming to drafting a five-paragraph essay.

GOING TO TEXT

Square 7 Once we have our story in our dummy book, we begin writing. On the first page is square 1 of the storyboard. Across from square 1 we tape a piece of paper to write on. We write what we told when we shared that square of our story. (Note: Do not have students write on the folded dummy page. Their text may need to be revised, so a removable sheet makes writing flexible for cut-and-paste.)

An example of the transition to text might go like this. Suppose a student is telling a story about a bear. To write her story in text, she needs only to look at her storyboard to know what to write. If her picture in square 1 shows a bear yawning, and the way she told it with square 1 was, "One morning a bear woke up. He was really grumpy and hungry. He wanted to punch somebody in the nose," then that's what she writes. The writing in this case is a text version of the telling.

MORE SHARING/REVISION

Square 8: Looking back at the handout for class picture books (page 89), you can see that square 8 is right below square 5. They look somewhat alike. Both squares show conferencing with an audience. The student here has written her whole story in text. Now she is ready to share again. She is ready to "tell-read" her story. Tell-reading is reading text out loud, but adding to the telling if something new pops out.

Square 9: In square 9, the tell-reading is done and the student is adding the suggestions the audience made to improve her writing. Notice the tongue sticking out. That's because text-writing is hard work, but this student is doing it because her audience told her she has to "tell" them the whole story.

The remaining four squares of this board show the simple steps in the publishing process. This is remarkably straightforward because students have created a small-scale dummy book that is a detailed blueprint for creating a larger book with formatted text and full-color illustrations. Of course the book-making process shown here—from idea to writing to making a working dummy book to creating a "published" work—exactly parallels the way a picture book is created for a book company.

Storyboard Telling: Oral Presentation

In a residency I did for a third-grade class, after kids had made finished picture books of their family stories, complete with amazing full-color illustrations and carefully edited text, they had a Family Stories Night for parents.

At this special event I watched a third grader explain the storyboarding writing process to an audience of 200. She used the bookmaking storyboard we just examined, enlarged on a big poster board. Pointing to each square,

she described all the steps kids used to make their picture books, "just like real authors and illustrators." Afterward, the speaker's mother came up, amazed at her daughter's new-found public-speaking skills. It was a powerful demonstration of the way storyboards support a speaker, square by square. Storyboards are, of course, a time-tested oral presentation tool, used in many adult settings, from engineering to "pitching a client" in advertising.

PICTURE WRITING BASICS

Since picture writing is new in most classrooms, and drawing as a thinking tool is also new, I keep my pictures basic. To help those nervous about drawing—students and teachers alike—I ask who can draw pictures "like a smart kindergartener." While teachers often worry about kids who can't/won't draw, I've seldom had a student who couldn't storyboard once he or she got the idea that *crummy pictures* are fine.

In a storyboard, we want very simple pictures that *communicate,* pictures that get the idea across easily. Storyboards need to be easy to draw, easy to read.

I often play a simplified version of the picture-drawing game Pictionary with the class before we storyboard. Asking students to communicate ideas in pure pictures is a great way to highlight symbol-making and to introduce basic image literacy. I start asking students to communicate straightforward ideas like "moose" and then try more abstract stuff like "lost." Of course, the more abstract the word, the more challenging the symbol-making and the funnier the results can be.

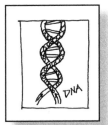

With older students who may see drawing as a "baby tool," I emphasize how sophisticated stick pictures are as a thinking tool. I show how simple pictures convey big ideas and suggest that some of the most important inventions first appeared as stick pictures on a napkin. If kids are skeptical, I show them the DNA helix, an abstract idea that is hard to discuss without simple pictures.

Key Words: Text and Picture Support Each Other

Actually, drawing on a storyboard is easier than playing Pictionary, because the rule is, if you can't draw it, then use a word. If you can't draw a moose the class can recognize, for example, then draw a stick animal and write the word "moose" under it. From then on in your storyboard, that stick

thing is always a moose. Text and pictures work together. If you need to show it was windy, add speed lines and write "wind." Now whenever those speed lines appear again, it means that it's windy again.

The drawing and text work together. If the writer has trouble drawing something and people ask, "What's that?" then all you have to do is add a key word to help out. If the thing you want people to know can't be drawn, use a key word. Uncle Fred is humming, for example, show his face and write, "humming." If Aunt Sally is stiff, a stick picture won't show that easily, so write "stiff." Above all, have fun getting the idea across in any way you can. Just as it is with storyboard drawing, you'll find the simpler the text, the better it works. And remember, fewer words are always better in a storyboard. A text-heavy storyboard can be hard to read.

Often students who draw well will leave out the key words. Reluctant writers may do that, too, but for other reasons. Students who draw well may think the pictures get the idea across by themselves, with no words necessary. Often they are right, but I tell them that we want pictures and words in every square, because some of us are good at reading pictures and some of us are good at reading text. So, if we put both text and pictures in every square of our storyboard, then everyone can read it. That, of course, encourages writers reluctant to attempt text to consider how words summarize ideas.

If the student got on a roller coaster, the key words might be, "got on coaster," or even "coaster," if the stick picture shows the figure climbing on. But if he was scared, we better have that be in the next square or add "scared" here. Key words communicate action and emotion.

A Few Important Rules

There are two rules I generally use when introducing storyboarding. These are designed to help everyone get started without fear.

1. **Drawing doesn't count.** That means bad drawings, simple stick pictures, are fine.
2. **Spelling doesn't count.** That means key words can be phonetic approximations as long as others know what you mean.

Most of the storyboards I use in the classroom are meant to be shared. That means the pictures or text should be readable, so that others can tell what you mean. Students show their storyboard to others to get feedback, so it is important they will not be ridiculed for poor drawing or poor spelling. These rules communicate that in storyboarding we are focusing on content; what does count is telling your story.

Spelling Note

Some teachers worry that saying "spelling doesn't count" is a problem. We know spelling is important on final drafts. But in my dyslexic bones I know that for a significant number of students, spelling is too hard, disabling enough to stop us from writing in the first place. I've seen writing "break-throughs" in too many classrooms to dismiss this rule. Does spelling count in the final drafts? Of course. But holding students accountable in first drafts stops many students from writing at all.

Not count spelling

Some of us spell easily; some struggle as I do, every time I write. Unfortunately, in school, spelling can be an issue disturbingly tinged with power. The good spellers make the rules. I know from working with lots of poor spellers that letting things roll and fixing the spelling later gets more effective writing. And it is less painful, too.

The "BBB" Rule

There's a third rule I tell kids for drawing on a storyboard. "Make your pictures BBB. That means BIG, **BOLD**, and BLACK."

The tiny figures in the left are two kids at the beach getting sunburned—there is lots of beach and sky. The second square is a close-up of those people filling the square. That's big, bold, and black.

The BBB rule is important for two reasons:

- A bold storyboard is easier to read. We want students to go for the main idea. Some children naturally draw tiny pictures, and for them this rule helps them to remember to "speak up." BBB also stops the detail freaks and the show-offs from getting carried away.
- When students share their storyboards, bigger pictures make it easier to see. That's important if we want folks in the back row to see what we have to say.

Using "Close-Ups" and Other Film Terms

Bold pictures will get the main idea across, and close-up pictures focus ideas more: If Mom is MAD, we don't need to see her legs. As I introduce storyboarding, I draw a lot of close-ups. These big faces convey basic emotions, reactions to events, and they bring more detail to the telling and the writing.

When I discuss students' storyboards I often use film terms like "close-ups" and "go to slo-mo" in a story. I talk about squares of a storyboard as if the writers were making a movie of their stories. I tell students that all movies are created in storyboards first: planned, plotted, and then fleshed out. Using film terms with writing makes that connection, and since students have seen many stories in movies, they find these terms comfortable and exciting.

Finding the Right Key Words

When we talked about pictures, we talked about BBB. The same idea holds true for key words. Tiny text is hard to read in a storyboard square. Think of key words as making headlines, words that get the main idea across. As we go on, you'll see that keywords can be used like close-ups in a drawing, as words become "loud."

Less Text Is Better—Think HEADLINES

When students share their boards, telling their story (or telling the life cycle of a cell), you will find too much text blocks a fluid telling. Storyboards dense with text are hard to share and hard to revise. We'll see in the next chapter how kids can get locked on their text. I usually tell students to use one, two, or three key words with an image.

Key words are most helpful when they move the telling forward by expressing action and emotion. Graphic writing will lead to more animated telling from a storyboard, and the better students tell their stories out loud,

the better they will tell them when they write text. It is hard to write a boring sentence about a big "OH, NO!"

Students new to key words may tend toward simple labels such as "roller coaster." Help them find key words that are more potent, words that speak to emotion or action. "Scary" and "gigantic" might appear. Students who use headlines are learning to summarize well. Strong key words point them toward better telling of the important ideas, strong emotions, and big reactions. Effective key words spur spontaneous story growth and more effective writing.

Storyboards are very powerful for learners with speech issues or those who get easily lost with abstract ideas. For them, key words need to be used carefully. Students who are very literal or rigid may get locked on potent key words. Finding the right words and putting them in the right order with the pictures from left to right will help unlock their spontaneous telling.

Draw and Laugh With Your Students

The best writing teachers say, "If you want students to write, write with them." The idea is to show kids we goof up when we write, too. The same

is true for drawing. Draw with your students and do it badly. Enjoy with them how funny and smart bad pictures can be. If your drawing is not recognizable, let students help; let everybody laugh at your dumb drawing of a dog. Let everybody discuss how to draw a dog that is more recognizable.

Time spent introducing basic drawing in stick pictures is never time wasted. Stick pictures can be fun and funny, but they are also a serious form of basic visual vocabulary. All students need to be able to communicate with image/ideas in our visual digital world. Students need to know that many great ideas in physics, math, architecture, or literature were first shared with stick pictures on a napkin or a blackboard. As you watch your students learn to use storyboards, you will see how stick pictures can convey amazingly sophisticated ideas.

CLASSROOM TOOLS: BASIC BOARDS

This is the first generic storyboard sheet I use with students. (See Appendix B, page 136, for a full-scale reproducible.) This layout with 13 squares is designed to let students get ideas on paper easily. The squares leave room to draw pictures and to write a few key text words. You'll notice the sheet could easily accommodate 15 squares, but I leave those two spaces empty to gives students a clear end square at the bottom.

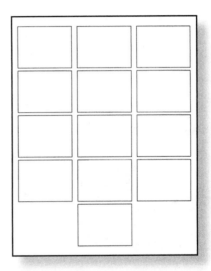

I prefer storyboard sheets that are the same size as standard writing paper so students' work fits into any folder or notebook. This conveys the idea that storyboards can be used for all kinds of writing. A teacher might say, "Grab a storyboard sheet to take notes." The sheet can be created with any standard word processor using drawing tools or it can be hand-drawn to give the idea that students can make their own sheets at home.

The tellingboard uses a larger 11-by-17-inch format that is easy to share with the class. For younger students, a larger size is easier to use.

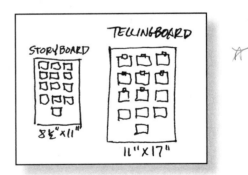

The Tellingboard: Real Cut-and-Paste Revision

Anyone who grew up writing without a word processor knows how different writing was before *cut-and-paste*. One of my big problems writing was that the ideas never came out of my head in the right order. The teacher's advice to "Just start writing" was always a mistake. I tried putting ideas on paper as they occurred to me and always ended up with a rambling

jumble. Like most kids, and about half the adults I know, text outlining never worked well either. I found once text got on paper, it seemed to solidify into a unit; everything locked together.

The first time I tried using cut-and-paste in a word processor I was in heaven. I took one sentence and moved it again and again, "seeing" how it "sounded" in each place. Suddenly I could learn to write without worrying what order the ideas came out of my head.

As you saw in Linda Rief's classroom, the tellingboard allows students to use a step-by-step picture-writing process, from brainstorming, through several drafts, to a final draft that makes the transition to text easy.

Working with a tellingboard gives students a true word/image processor with intuitive cut-and-paste capability that can rival the computer for no-fault revision, yet this tool fits in the writing folder and costs almost nothing.

When young writers find they can easily move things and try a new order for their story, and when they can see the results of the change immediately and clearly, then the abstract process starts to makes sense.

We will see in Chapter 8 how this moveable storyboard actually spurs revision. The ability to literally move parts of stories confirms on a deeper level the idea that a writer constructs with ideas. As students take cards and move them, then retell their stories, they will be doing the nuts-and-bolts work of the writer: learning to construct a clear story, and then learning to take it apart and fix it. For advanced writers struggling with complex plot, the storyboard encourages experimentation and makes them more confident changing their work.

Tellingboards are versatile sequencing tools with many applications for the classroom. They are also a great hands-on way to introduce high-tech writing skills like creating a PowerPoint presentation, without all the high-tech hassles. Like writing, the hands-on experience of constructing a presentation on cards, in words and images, which can be moved to revise ideas once the student receives feedback, focuses the student on communicating. The resulting presentation is more focused and effective, whether using simple stick-pics or translating them into whiz-bang digital graphics.

MAKING A TELLINGBOARD TEMPLATE

This tellingboard is a larger version of the basic 13-square storyboard sheet I introduced earlier, with moveable cards placed in the squares. As the name implies, the tellingboard is designed to be a sharing tool. Students tell their story from the board to the whole class.

The tellingboard is the size of an open file folder. It holds 13 half-size standard file cards, each attached with a small hinge of tape. File cards are taped lightly onto the squares, as shown below. When the board is folded closed, it fits in the student's standard writing folder. When open, it is big enough to read from the back of a classroom.

You can use file folders or 11-by-17 stock. The basic 13 storyboard squares can be drawn in with a marker on each board, but it is easier to draw one template on the 11-by-17-inch board that will fit a copy machine. Then a class set of boards can be copied on heavy stock. The cards I generally use are standard 3-by-5-inch file cards cut in half on a paper cutter. Get plenty of extra cards; if they come in packs of 500, you will produce 1,000 cards.

I do not recommend sticky notes, especially with younger kids. We want them to feel their work is substantial. Sticky notes are temporary; this is permanent. If they take cards away in revision, they can save them in an envelope. These are story ideas they might use later, so they don't feel they wasted time making them.

A small piece of tape, one inch sideways across the top of the card like a hinge, will hold the card in place, but allow it to be picked off easily, moved, and stuck on again. Make sure card squares fall above or below the fold. Cards are not supposed to get bent when the folder is closed.

Each kid gets a manila folder to store storyboard

Experiment w/ artists tape

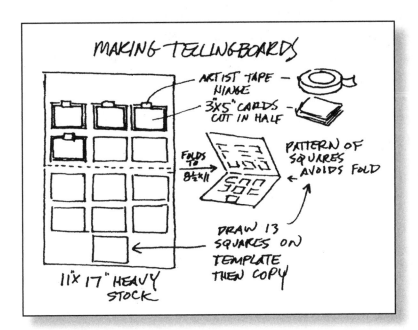

Chapter 8

Shared Writing: Revision and Conferencing Made Simple

Linda Rief has shown us how Shared Writing engaged her reluctant writers, and how group revision and conferencing was easier for everyone, including her. Jim Doherty told us Shared Reading in an upper-elementary classroom makes the inclusion of special education students in time-strapped classrooms both practical and effective. Their common experience—that low-text collaborative strategies engage *all* learners and save time—is no small potatoes.

Students will show teachers experienced with traditional text strategies how these different tools change the learning landscape by connecting learners in a way text alone can't. In this chapter we'll explore how teaching writing as a collaborative process with the whole class allows students to take more responsibility for both their writing and revision. We'll also explore how connecting writers with an audience creates a writing community that pulls all learners into the literacy circle.

REVISION AND CONFERENCING STANDOFFS

Anyone who works with young writers knows revision can be tough. We've all heard, "But I already wrote it!" as the default reaction to any suggestion that a student's writing might be improved. Revision often creates an immediate classroom divide. Kids will tell you, "No matter what I write, the teacher always wants me to change it." Teachers will tell you, "No matter what I say, many kids don't want to revise. They think just getting words on paper is the end of the process."

Teaching writing as a collaborative process that connects writer and audience makes sense on lots of levels. For too many students, good and reluctant writers alike, writing in school is a lonely experience with no payoff beyond a grade.

Even for kids comfortable with text, we know that writing with no sense of audience is trouble. We've all seen the symptoms: "good writers" in a class proudly reading pages of text as their captive audience squirms, bored to tears. Those "productive" young writers have been fooled into believing that putting words on paper is the goal of writing. We tell young writers that to communicate effectively they need to imagine their audience. That's a tall order even for advanced writers. The natural strength of Shared Writing is that it connects the writer with a real audience of peers.

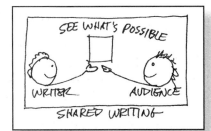

What's more, many teachers tell me they feel they lack the expertise for conferencing. Good teachers ask me, "How can I be sure I'm giving students good feedback?" From the teacher's point of view, connecting a writer with a real audience can diffuse conferencing/revision standoffs that can seem endless and inevitable. Other teachers who have tried peer conferencing say, "Kids aren't great at giving feedback and it's hard to teach them how to ask good questions or give valuable suggestions." Students can show us how to conference more effectively when we teach them how to use storyboards to guide that response.

Let me try to show the lively excitement of the Shared Writing process. We'll follow a teller and her audience as they grapple with the messy business of story building and revision. We'll see a girl's story literally get "ripped apart" and then rebuilt in one class session.

You'll see how connecting a writer with her audience changes the conferencing dynamic, allowing the teacher to play a less loaded role. At the same time I hope to show how drawing and telling, as casual non-text tools, change the way students respond to one another's hard work. I have learned from students that sharing a draft storyboard is fundamentally different from sharing a text draft of a story. Understanding that difference is key to understanding why storyboards make revision easier and more engaging for many young writers.

SHARING HOOKS: WRITER AND AUDIENCE ENGAGE

It was a crowded fourth-grade classroom, 50 kids from two classes packed in. Most were sitting on the floor, but in the back they were sitting on top of desks that had been shoved out of the way. Also in the back were classroom teachers and several other adult observers who had dropped in to watch.

All the kids in the fourth grade had collected family stories. I was starting to engage writers with their audience by having them share their hooks. There had been lots of good hooks, crowd-pleasers like "My brother crashed the car" and "My dad jumped off the shed roof . . . into the manure pile." We gave those tellers the immediate nod to start putting a full first draft on a storyboard.

Then Katie came forward to share her hook. It was obvious when Katie volunteered that she thought she had a good hook; she was grinning and waving at me. Katie was still grinning when she said, "My hook is that my dad found the cheapest motel on the Internet."

Katie beamed and waited for her audience to react. Their looks said, "Big deal." Katie turned to me, confused. She felt she had a hook, and I was pretty sure she did, but I knew she was missing a critical step in the writing process. Katie felt she had a good story, she was ready to write, but her audience was telling her to think again.

First Essential Revision: Finding the Full Hook

Katie was stuck, but she was getting a timely heads-up. If your target audience doesn't think you have a hook, you better find out why before you start writing. Unfortunately, many young writers only learn what their audience thinks after their "finished" story bombs. Then the students often learn the wrong lesson: They learn they are bad writers.

In this Shared Writing process, I encourage students to take the lead in revision. Getting the teacher out of the lone writing expert role, and connecting a writer with his or her audience, makes revision real. And group conferencing allows everyone to learn how a story might grow.

I have come to see my job in conferences as a referee, setting up safe ground rules that allow the teller and audience to connect. When things are moving forward, I get out of the way. But in this case, I thought I could help Katie (and her audience) figure out what she was missing. I asked Katie, "Was the motel bad?" She grinned, lit up again, and said, "Oh, YEAH! It was a real dump."

Kids still didn't react, but she had me; I could already picture the bare lightbulb in the dingy motel. Fishing for drama, I said, "Is there a mom in this story?"

She said, "Yessss," and her grin got gigantic. Now all the teachers in back laughed. They knew Katie had a hook if Mom and Dad are at odds. Still, Katie's target audience, her peers, were frowning, not sure what was funny, not convinced Katie had a hook for them.

Sharing Everything: The Mouse Appears

So far, Katie had not completely shared her hook. Maybe she was unsure of what she had, or perhaps she was offering her version of a traditional opening. Students (and adults) who've learned writing conventions often misunderstand the goal in sharing a hook. They offer a taste of what's to come. They might say, "When something happened to my uncle's airplane." These writers have learned to save the best part of the story so they don't give it away prematurely. But in Shared Writing we are trying to give the story away. You try to tell your audience the best you've got, so they can tell you what they really think, so they can help you grow your ideas.

Making a Movie

I asked, "What's the best part of your story?" She frowned at me. I said, "What's the most exciting thing that happens? If we're making a movie of your story, which part does everybody want to see?"

Katie brightened and said, "When my dad killed the mouse with his shoe?" Finally, her audience came alive. When someone asked if he actually squished it, she nodded, beaming. Kids made disgusted faces, others laughed. Katie had her hook. In fact, Katie had a family gem with two hooks: a good bloody hook for the kids, and a funny marriage drama to please the adults.

Katie's audience told her to get to work storyboarding, and they told her what they wanted to see and hear more about—that mouse! Katie's first draft storyboard was on a small sheet, filling in as many squares as she thought it took. That first draft grew when she had transferred her story to a tellingboard, putting the events on cards for easier sharing and revision.

Katie's First Full Telling

The room was packed again when Katie came forward to share her full story. As I taped her tellingboard to my easel, I saw she had a good clear board. She had used all 13 cards and she had bold pictures and bold text. She smiled at me, ready.

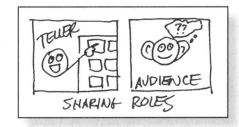

I quieted the crowd down, and pointing to the two stick-pics (shown here) that I'd drawn on my easel, I reminded everybody that the class is divided into two roles now, the teller and the audience. I explained, "The teller's job is to tell her story clearly, pointing to the squares so everyone knows where she is. The job of the audience (you folks) is to listen carefully and to watch for questions that pop into your

Katie's first full draft of her "Cheapest Motel" story

head. Those questions will help us discuss Katie's telling after she has finished." I also reminded Katie to "read" the squares on her board carefully, telling everything she thought was important. Then I stepped to the side, and the telling began.

As Katie pointed to her first card, a picture of her dad at the computer, she said, "My dad got on the Internet and he told us he found the cheapest motel for our vacation." She pointed to the next card, "We all packed . . ." Her story got off to a slow start. She told us all about the stuffed car, the details of what chips and drinks they got when they stopped at a 7-Eleven, the long boring drive, and so forth. By the time they got to the motel parking lot, we were on square 8, and her audience was restless and sick of the trip.

Finally, at square 10, Katie told us about Mom seeing their crummy room with only bunk beds. (The cheapest motel on the Internet was one that used old summer-camp cabins.) She had three squares left when everyone was tucked in, and the mouse came out of the wall. Square 11: Mom woke screaming. Now everybody laughed. Square 12: Dad killed the mouse with his shoe—lots of squeals. Square 13 (the last): The mouse was deposited in the trash behind the motel. Done.

Falling Into the "It's Good" Trap

As Katie finished, she looked at me for a reaction. We all tried to be nice. I asked what the rest of the students thought of her story. Several polite kids said, "It's good." This was a typical "helpful" response to writing, and a deadly one. It means we heard it, now let's move on. But Katie's audience owed her more than that.

I turned to her, smiled, and winked with one eye so only she could see. I said low, "Stay with me." Katie nodded. I said, "Your story is perfect! I wouldn't change a word of it." She frowned. Everybody stared at me. I asked, "What's wrong?"

Someone said, "You lied to her." Lots of nods. They looked at me, outraged.

I said, "I did lie, didn't I? I just did the meanest thing you can do to someone when they share a story. I lied." They frowned at my cruel dishonesty. I asked, "What could I say about her story if I was being honest?"

Good News: Everyone's a Critic

A girl said tentatively, "It's a little boring." A ripple of nods followed. They all looked at Katie to see how she was going to react. Katie, looking tentative as well, said, "I thought it was a little boring, too." I could tell she was surprised to discover what seemed fine on paper and in her head came off as boring in front of a real audience.

I asked, "How many people think it's a good story, but it could be more exciting?" All hands went up, including Katie's. She was looking a little worried, but I reminded her of a central idea of Shared Writing. I pointed at all the raised hands and said, "This is great. Look how many people want to help. If they don't like your story, then it's their problem to offer some ideas about how to fix it."

This was not intended as a cute way to soften the criticism. I was trying to show that Katie needs criticism. She did her best to tell her story, and before she shared it, it sounded fine to her. Then her audience said, "It's not working." How can she fix it if she doesn't know what's wrong? It is her audience's responsibility to tell her what's wrong. Connecting writers with a real audience is essential, but I've seen that connection derailed when students have been told their reactions must be "positive."

Critics Become Peer Editors

Katie was learning that collaboration means she's not in this alone; her audience was ready to be a full partner in building her story. My job was to model for that audience how to be good listeners and sensitive editors. I focused the team conference by asking, "What is the hook in Katie's story? What's the most exciting part?"

A girl said, "When the mouse comes out of the wall." Everybody nodded. I asked her to get up and go point to that square on Katie's board. She pointed to square 11. We added a hook to that square.

I asked, "Where does the story first get interesting?"

Someone said not until they got to the motel. Everybody could see that was a long way, not until square 8. That's the thing; on a storyboard everybody can scan, see in concrete terms how many squares it takes for the story to get going.

A storyboard serves as a visual diagram of the story that allows concrete, inclusive revision discussion between author and audience.

With that hint from me, a student asked, "Couldn't they get to the motel in square two or three?" Lots of voices said, "Yeah!" I smiled now. Katie's audience had gone from a dismissive "It's good," to asking real editorial questions that help the writer see how her story might grow. Seeing students grasp the responsibility for editing is exciting. Teachers are often amazed that students engaged by a story will ask the same questions the teacher might, but with a big difference: Focused questions coming from peers have a lot more impact. Writers can see why they need to revise—their audience wants more.

Teacher Going Overboard

Excited by their revision breakthrough, and hoping to model how a tellingboard easily advances revision, I did something dumb. I reached over and pulled cards 3–9 off Katie's board. I handed them to her saying, "Save these cards in an envelope labeled 'Road Trip Story.' I especially like the way your sister has to go pee all the time, but here we all want to know more about the motel and the mouse."

Then turning back to the board I moved the "got to motel" card up to square 3 saying, "Try having your family arrive here." I pointed down at the last square, "We know that mouse is dead here." Pointing to the now empty middle squares I said, "We know the mouse comes out somewhere in here. Tell us everything. Build up to the mouse, and then tell us what happens after he comes out of the wall."

I was suggesting this rearranged board was a revision diagram, showing everyone where the story might grow, but when I turned to Katie, her upset look stopped me. I realized I hadn't asked her about pulling her board apart in front of the whole class. Hoping for the best I said, "Do you think you can add squares, tell your story better?"

Katie seemed torn, not sure if she'd been wronged by the sudden cuts. I leaned close and said, "If you'll rebuild the story, add cards to tell it better, you can come back up here in a few minutes and tell it again."

Katie's story is pulled apart; the empty squares create a blueprint for revision.

There was a long moment as she looked at the board to see what was left. Then she said, "Okay," with enough confidence that I thought she had seen how to rebuild. Her audience smiled at Katie's decision. I breathed again, glad for her resilience. We got her some new cards, and she went to the back of the room with her tellingboard.

Revision Notes

Katie had to see how her story might grow before she could revise it. If Katie had seemed unsure, had she said "maybe," as some kids do, I would have asked her to pick several partners to help her rebuild her board. I've now learned that tellers need to have a note-taker to make "revision notes" for them during group conferencing. Each time folks agree a new square is needed, the note-taker (a student, or the teacher in earlier grades) makes a storyboard note. Often the note-taker will help the student review and revise his or her board when the telling/sharing is done.

Telling the Full Story

When Katie came back up front 20 minutes later, she had completely revised her board. Her telling got off to a breezy start with Dad "announcing" his find on the Internet. The trip began in square 2. Square 3 was the arrival at the motel, and here Katie had added lots of detail, like seeing the empty pool as they went in. We got a good tour of the crummy bedroom and the moldy bathroom. Katie added "When I saw the hole in the wall by the refrigerator, my dad told me not to tell." Katie said, "Did I tell you my mom is really scared of mice?"

Katie's revised storyboard with new squares offers a view of the full motel disaster.

Everybody laughed, and they could see Katie had added lots of new stuff. This is common. When students have more squares available, and they know what their audience wants to know, they suddenly remember more of the story. In her new telling, Katie said both her sister and her mom are terrified of mice, and in square 8, Katie said her mom climbed up on the top bunk bed and screamed with the sister as Dad chased that mouse around for three squares, throwing his shoe at it, diving across the bed, and breaking a lamp before we all squirmed as he squished that injured mouse. The story still ended with the mouse going into the trash can.

Editors Again

We all laughed and clapped. I had to wait for the kids to settle down before we could see what they thought of her revised story. I asked for editor questions. The first was, "What happened? Did you stay at that motel or leave?" It was a question I hadn't thought of, and it immediately took Katie's story beyond the mouse to her second important hook.

Katie said, "I forgot. My mom was so mad she made my dad take us to the most expensive hotel in town. It had a pool and a hot tub." The room

erupted with laughter. Everyone agreed this was a great ending to her story; Katie needed to add two squares, one of fun in the hot tub, another of everybody splashing Dad in the pool.

With those two squares, Katie's story brought her two hooks together, the mouse and the adult conflict easily woven into a hilarious ending, and Katie and her audience were together, too. Now she was ready to go to text—knowing everybody wanted the whole story.

Very Different Drafts

As class ended I marveled at what Katie and her audience had accomplished: In perhaps 20 minutes Katie had shared, discussed, dismantled, rebuilt, expanded, and retold her story—and brought the house down.

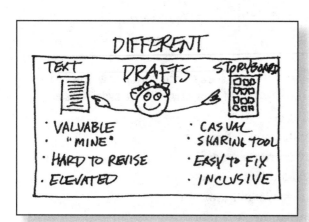

At the time I felt Katie's resilient comeback, after having her story ripped apart, was remarkable good luck. I know now I'd seen a practical demonstration of the way sharing storyboard drafts and sharing text drafts is fundamentally different for students. Katie's class demonstrated the way drawing and telling with an engaged audience clears a pathway through typical revision roadblocks.

Any teacher familiar with the phrase, "But I already wrote it!" can imagine how Katie's story might have fared if Katie had already written a text draft. Imagine the same words read aloud from two pages of text: a full page of "road trip," the second page ending with several paragraphs about the motel and the mouse. Now imagine after reading aloud, her peers, or her teacher, telling her that the whole first page of her story was "kinda boring." If you can see her moving past that first barrier, then imagine the discussion, how she might start over, revise, rewrite, and share again 15 minutes later.

Watching the spontaneous exchange in Shared Writing with low-text tools offers valuable insight into the way text itself can block writing and revision. Students have shown me that text itself has a weight and importance that makes it hard to discuss, hard to criticize honestly. Further text, even a draft, can feel "done." I still have nightmare images of my papers coming back from the teacher, with crossed-out or circled text and scary arrows zooming around the page.

My experience with Shared Writing tells me that Katie's story can be easily expanded and revised precisely because she has not written it in weighty, valuable text yet.

Collaborative Writing Saves Time

One of the most obvious benefits of collaborative writing is that conference and revision with the whole class means everyone has a stake in the revision, and we can all see what works and what does not. That means everyone learns more.

Many kids feel they write for no one, or for an audience of one, the teacher. Adult writers often look to an audience. They join a writers' group where they can share work in progress, get feedback, and discuss problems. But there is another reason writers' groups come together. At heart, all writers want to connect. Having an engaged audience is the payoff for all the hard work.

Students show us that teachers alone are no substitute for the real engagement of a peer audience. Students rightly perceive the teacher as a biased observer. "The teacher always wants more writing." When the audience asks for more from a writer, or says that a writer's story needs work, these reactions carry authentic weight that makes revision relevant and worth doing.

The good news is students will take responsibility for their writing choices if we give them a process that looks easy and logical. They will also teach each other, and show us that writing, even revising, is worth all the hard work when we know others want to hear what we have to say. Students from whom no one expected much have taught me that exciting writing comes from collaboration in an engaged writing community where all learners are pulled into the writing circle.

Shared Writing: The Essential Writers Group

As I clipped my portable microphone to Ramon's T-shirt, he looked at me like I'd betrayed him. I'd been surprised when his story was chosen for

Family Story Night. Just reading out loud would be hard for him, but I had told him it would be "no big deal, just a small audience like he was used to in class." Nobody had said anything about using a microphone, because nobody had expected this big crowd. As he stepped forward, I knew he'd written a good story, but I also knew how scared he was. Ramon was not the kind of student a school usually chooses to highlight its literacy program. I suspected he had never volunteered to read aloud in front of his class, much less to half the school.

I'd been invited to this struggling inner-city school to see if low-text tools could get more kids writing. Teachers had warned me that motivating these kids

would be tough—reading and writing were not part of their regular home lives. Just getting a family story from home would be hard. But the students got great stories from home and embraced drawing and telling as tools for building, revising, and writing solid stories. The teachers' commitment was impressive, too. At the end of the process, each student had written and illustrated a full-blown picture book of his or her family story.

But when I suggested we celebrate everyone's hard work with an evening family event, teachers balked. They'd said I didn't understand this kind of poor community school; parents didn't come to school events. I wasn't surprised some folks avoided school. Kids at the bottom of the literacy pile often have parents who've been at the bottom themselves. Still I pushed; family stories ought to be shared with families. When I asked if the school got a good turnout for any school event, the teachers said Free Pizza Night was popular.

On Family Story Night, the cafeteria was so packed the principal had to send out for additional pizzas. Ramon, the first author to read, stepped up.

He held his picture book up over his head so folks on the far side could see the cover. Then he opened it and started reading. Immediately, he stumbled. Ramon paused to hold up his first picture. Only those in front could see his carefully drawn illustrations. Still, the pause got Ramon settled, and as he read about his grandpa crawling in the mud toward the machine-gun nest, the crowd focused. When he got to the part about his grandpa dragging his buddy out of the line of fire, there wasn't a sound. Ramon's classmates smiled, watching adults crane their necks to see a fellow writer.

Ramon's class was proud of his story. They'd liked it right from the start when Ramon shared his hook, "When My Grandpa Saved His Friend From a Machine-Gun." Ramon's classmates knew every square of his story; they all helped him build it, discussing how to add suspense and barbed wire detail to make it realistic and scary.

But I don't think they had heard that the hero of the story was in the room that night. Ramon's teacher had pointed him out to me, a guy standing alone in back by the doors. Grandpa looked uncomfortable at the reading, as if he might be an old reluctant writer himself. I suspect as he watched his grandson reading to everyone, he knew how much courage that took.

When Ramon finished reading, he looked up and beamed. But he wasn't the only one; his classmates beamed, too, and shoved each other, soaking in the crowd's whistles and hoots and genuine applause. They had reason to be proud; Ramon's story grabbed the larger audience because his classmates had been willing to be his first engaged audience.

A Shared Writing classroom builds what I call a telling circle, where ideas are safely shared and refined before anyone has to commit to text. For sure, Ramon did not work alone. He found he could build his story by collaborating with his peers, taking turns as teller and audience, both roles essential to any writer's process. When Ramon finally wrote text, he did it with confidence, because his peers had told him his story was ready to be written.

ENABLING TRUE DIVERSITY

I hoped Ramon's classmates would get to meet his grandpa after this evening, maybe invite him in to tell a few more stories. The telling circle they had created in their classroom would grow to include lots of new tellers, folks from the larger community who brought more stories and more inspired writing.

Discovering how low-text drawing and telling connect and support writers opens the door to a more inclusive view of literacy, one that connects diverse learners. The concrete visual sharing of a storyboard format can bridge wide gaps in literacy and language, connecting folks who value a good story.

Chapter 9

"Different" Learners in the Visual Classroom

It was at the end of the class when Donald volunteered to get up and share his storyboard, and we had already heard lots of good first-draft stories. Donald came forward, moving awkwardly, self-conscious and nervous. His storyboard looked awkward, too: maybe six squares with weak repetitive pictures, no close-ups or dramatic events visible, and few strong key words either.

I'd been invited to Donald's school by the seventh-grade language arts team who told me that most of the students did not consider writing "cool." They had lots of reluctant writers, but they were hopeful that Shared Writing might get more kids going. I didn't know anything about Donald, but as he started telling, I wondered why he had volunteered. His basic story was supposed to be a comedy, a series of minor fishing mishaps, but his stiff and halting telling killed the humor. Before he was halfway through, I saw kids smirking and rolling their eyes. By the time he got to the good part, about a big fish swallowing the small fish on his line, he'd lost his audience.

When he finished, I asked if anyone had any questions, my usual way to get kids reacting to a story. They said nothing. I had encouraged honest reactions and let the kids carry the ball, until now. These kids had been engaged, their reactions on target and helpful. The silence was mean. I wasn't sure what Donald's history was, but he didn't seem to have any friends here.

I had to intervene. I told Donald he had built a solid story, one that needed to be expanded, but that it was a good start. Then I turned to his class and asked what they thought. I saw their skeptical looks. I repeated strongly that it was a good story, but that comedy was the hardest kind of story to tell well. I told them if they wanted to learn how to do comedy, they needed to help Donald make his story funny.

They tried. Everybody agreed his hook was losing that big fish. But we agreed it wasn't funny alone; he needed to work on his buildup, show his full day of bad luck in a more dramatic way, and play up all his goofs. I drew a close-up of a face: hair on end, mouth and eyes wide, amazed at the size of the fish that got away.

I knew simple pictures would be his comic allies; bad stick pictures are funny. As the class ended, I wondered how much of that Donald had gotten. Our sharing was too rushed, and I wasn't hopeful. I doubted he could make a good, funny book.

HELPING ALL STUDENTS

When I introduce Shared Writing in a school, I rarely get to see the whole process. My work usually takes kids through conferencing and revision, then the classroom teacher takes over, and kids' final transition to text happens after I'm gone. At this school, however, the teachers had invited me back to see kids share their finished picture books.

There were too many good books for me to see, and there were lots of hands up when I asked who wanted to read last. I'd told the teacher to signal me if there were kids who might not normally share, and she pointed to Donald. The sad truth is I didn't want Donald to read. I didn't want him to bomb again, but what could I do?

He got up and stumbled forward. I crossed my fingers for him.

As he began showing the first picture, I was surprised to see a big, colorful cartoon. It wasn't sophisticated art, but it was clear he had worked hard on his drawings. His writing was basic, just a few sentences per page, but it did the job. He'd come a long way. Still, his reading aloud was slow and awkward. Just a few pages into his story, kids were glancing at each other; he was losing them again. I went up front and said, "I like this story. Let me try reading it to show how to read comedy." He looked relieved. I started reading, a little nervous myself. No one here knew I'd avoided all opportunities to read aloud in front of people until I was 45 years old.

As I read his story and paused to show the pictures, I put some drama in my voice, and kids started laughing. But it wasn't me. As the story continued, Donald's dramatic/comic self-portraits, close-ups of his over-the-top reactions to events, were really funny. As the disasters accumulated and then that big fish got away, we were all laughing. When I was done reading, he faced the class and beamed, while everybody clapped. They meant it.

Including All Writers

After all the kids left, the teacher and I talked about how well her reluctant writers had done. She was enthusiastic, discussing a number of kids who'd engaged and done work that surprised her. But when I asked if she thought Donald's writing was better than his usual work, she said, "I don't know."

I was confused. I said, "I was just trying to figure out if you thought storyboards helped him write."

She said, "The thing is, he's not really in my class. I don't really know anything about his writing. He's Special Ed. He's not mainstreamed in Language Arts. When we started planning this residency, I asked, 'What about Donald?' We don't normally see him, but we decided since storyboarding was different, maybe he could do it, too. We decided to put him in my room to see how it went."

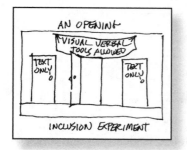

Donald was not mainstreamed. That explained so much. Then she said something I'll never forget: "The kids don't think of him as part of this class, really. I'm afraid some of them make fun of him behind his back. But I saw them looking at him today, as you read his story. I saw kids looking at him differently. I think they were reevaluating who he is, because his story was good, really funny."

We adults have so much power. We can make "different" students disappear. Unfortunately, Donald's classmates had help evaluating him. They learned from adults how different he was. Adults made it clear Donald couldn't be part of a normal class, at least not using traditional tools. The good news is kids are adaptable; they can change their assessment of someone like Donald, often more quickly than we adults can.

Throughout this book, we've seen kids respond to a low-text reading and writing process with dramatic breakthroughs. These breakthroughs often appear dramatic because in a text-only classroom, such students are held back, unable to show what they know.

Donald volunteered to share twice. That took guts few of his classmates could match, but I think he wanted to make a statement. "Different" learners have taught me this: Many of us become different when adults insist we learn with tools that don't work well for us.

I know those Language Arts teachers took the first big step toward Donald: "We decided since storyboarding was *different*, maybe he (Donald) could do it, too." The decision to offer kids drawing and telling as writing tools in the Language Arts classroom was courageous. So was including Donald. Kids like Donald seldom get the chance to show what they can do with comfortable tools. Special Ed teachers know their kids want to be successful and included, but school structure and text focus can make those goals seem at odds and hard to achieve.

"Learning Disabled" Vs. "Text Disabled"

Mel Levine has written persuasively about the way adults too easily marginalize different learners, as the title of his book, *The Myth of Laziness* (2003), implies. Too often adults find it easier to label kids as weak learners than to ask themselves hard questions about learning. There is plenty of evidence that using labels like "learning disabled" is dangerous business. As a legal term it is necessary and useful, but as an education label it can send an unfortunate message: We adults know how to teach; this is the learner's problem alone.

When parents are told at the evaluation meeting, "Your child has a learning disability; she is having difficulty with the essential text skills central for success in school," that's when they feel the bottom dropping out. Any teacher who has attended one of these meetings knows how difficult they are. Still, the teacher whose own child is labeled will tell you that teachers have no idea how powerless parents feel until they've sat on the "disabled" side of the table.

"Learning disabled" is useful shorthand in some contexts, but it can also be used to justify a powerful one-way judgment, delivered in a neat clinical package. Yet anyone who has seen an effective teacher and a poor one teach the same material knows education is always a complex, two-way process. I propose we try an experiment. Let's redefine learning problems related to text and see what we might discover. I'm not playing a word game. I'm proposing these labels can color our thinking, skewing our view of the child and of the problem at hand.

Examining learning problems related to text might be more fruitful if we say, "text disables," as in, "We know as educators that text disables a significant number of kids, despite our best interventions." Saying "text disables" has many advantages over labeling the kids themselves. First, it allows us to describe an education problem we know is complicated without blaming anyone, especially kids who can't argue with our judgment. Second, it allows us the flexibility to consider that the difficulty we have teaching text might be central to many learning problems. I find when we adults open that door, the fresh scent of possibility blows through the long-closed room.

Pretend for a moment we've recognized text as a block to learning, and we've devised alternative visual/verbal tools that we know work for reluctant readers and writers. I want to suggest how different our conversations might be with parents. "Your child is having difficulty with text skills. We find text is disabling to many perfectly competent learners. We will need to be sure the way we teach includes easy-to-use low-text tools that will not turn this small text setback into a big one." Notice in that conversation no child is labeled or blamed and that educators are identifying a problem they can take responsibility for and address.

UNDERSTANDING STUDENT DIFFERENCES

In his work on multiple intelligences, Armstrong (2000) noted the origins of written language in pictures and highlighted the ability of all children to learn with picture-symbol languages more easily than with text. He noted that the Japanese is one of several modern languages that has kept a connection to pictures, in the script known as Kanji. He asserts that in Japan, "reading disabilities are rare" as a result of students learning two basic alphabets, a text language and a picture script (p. 105).

Armstrong reinforced his assertion that it's the picture connections that help cut reading disabilities as he described the work of psychologists Paul Rozin, Susan Porisky, and Raina Sotsky, who taught inner city kids "with severe [text] difficulties" by using Chinese picture characters to represent English and found: "Children who had failed to master English alphabet sounds in over one year and a half of schooling immediately understood the basic demands of the task and were able to read sentences in five or ten minutes of exposure to Chinese" (ibid).

We do know picture symbols make sense to kids—a stick man is easy for preliterate kids to recognize—but abstract text is just disabling gibberish without serious work learning to decode. Armstrong's idea takes on greater weight when we look at Donald Graves' work (also mentioned in Chapter 2), which showed that pictures make intuitive sense to kids as a way to build meaning, in reading or writing. Indeed, Graves found drawing was kids' first writing/thinking tool, and their natural bridge to text.

Understanding that text sometimes disables and that pictures work for everyone allows us as educators to find common ground with our text-slow learners. Considering text as an abstract disabler and recognizing how concrete pictures support all learners allows us to examine how diverse learning problems and classroom difficulties are related.

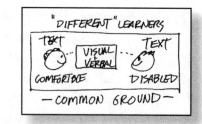

We've all observed the learning struggles that stem from the exacting nature of text as abstract code—problems with decoding, sequencing, memory, and comprehension are common text issues. Other classroom learning problems are shown to be more language-based problems: following verbal instruction or class discussion and responding to verbal questions. Again, memory, sequencing, and comprehension are involved. We've seen how storyboards address all these problems, how concrete, sequenced pictures are the antidote to many text and verbal issues.

Special Education—Isolating the Problems

The focus of this book has been helping kids in the mainstream class-room because that's where visual/verbal tools will have the most impact for students, learning disabled or not. Using visual tools only in Special Ed just continues the segregated learning.

A text-dominated curriculum puts text-challenged kids at an immediate disadvantage. Special Education was designed to address this problem. Unfortunately, when we discover a student is struggling, we usually cannot provide a mainstream alternative to text. Indeed, many Special Ed accommodations assume our text-focused education curriculum is inevitable, and that kids just have to suffer through it.

Parents of students who struggle tell me how frustrating it is to find that books aimed at helping them support their children in school highlight the ways narrow text-focused instruction can make learning too hard. Yet these same books seem to assume educators cannot (or will not) change the tools they offer. Common advice to parents puts the burden back on the students, offering strategies to help different learners "work around" the traditional curriculum.

Ironically, many solutions suggested for kids with "learning problems" actually require the disabled student to work twice as hard to overcome "their problems" by being super learners—learning with tools that don't suit them, *working around* the text-only blocks we put in front of them.

The general thrust of much Special Education or remedial work is often an effort to intensify the text instruction in a special class or with a special tutor. While this sometimes helps, it is often disruptive and stigmatizing, not to mention labor-intensive and expensive.

It also may be the last thing we should do. Let's pretend that a text-slow child is comparable to a child allergic to milk. Our current solution to this al-

lergy is to prescribe a text-rich diet: text drills, tutors, worksheets, text homework—all intended to get the student past his problem. In effect, we have the milk-allergic child drinking milk morning, noon, and night with extra milk at bedtime, too, if the parents will help with the force feeding.

Once we glimpse how effectively verbal/visual tools help teach literacy skills, then our current learning logic sounds suspiciously circular. In effect, adults say, "Kids learn best with text, so we will teach mostly in text. Therefore, students who have trouble with text have, by default, a "learning disability."

Certainly our current approach to Special Ed often diminishes perceptions of children's learning potential. The "different" learner too easily becomes the "other" for text-comfortable students and adult learners. Too often the Special Ed path has many disturbing shades of separate-but-equal education. The irony is that finding tools that benefit the text-disabled learners often results in increased learning for all kids.

Jake Speaks

When a teacher who has seen a storyboarding workshop tells me, "I can see how this is a great extra technique, one any teacher could keep in their back pocket," I think of Jake, who taught me I had too narrow a view of storyboards as a learning tool. And more importantly, I had too narrow a view of Jake as a learner.

I wasn't invited to Jake's school to work with him. I'd been invited by the seventh-grade Language Arts teachers to introduce storyboarding as a mainstream writing tool. During my morning break, I'd dropped by the Special Ed room to ask if they could think of kids at other grade levels who had serious issues who might benefit from storyboarding. The teacher thought for a few moments before she said, "Maybe Jake?"

I followed directions through a hall filled with first-grade pictures and out of the building. I stepped into the speech trailer and explained to the

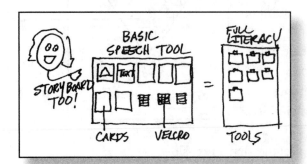

teacher what I was doing with the seventh-grade classes. She immediately got the idea. She showed me basic storyboards used as speech therapy tools, Velcro squares with words and symbols used to sequence sentences. This teacher immediately saw how this familiar tool might become a sophisticated writing tool.

She said, "Let me get Jake," and went into the next room.

Jake was a big eighth grader, pleasant looking; he could easily fit in, until he spoke. It took me a couple of sentences before I could understand a word he said. By that time I was wondering if I could politely admit to his teacher I'd made a mistake suggesting he try storyboarding as a learning tool.

I tried to explain I was there to show him storyboarding. He listened with intense laser focus, but his facial expression gave me no clue if he understood a word I said. When I asked him, "Do you like to draw?" there was a long pause, but he kept urgent eye contact that said, "Wait, wait!" I had the feeling I was watching a powerful inner struggle, like a silent stutter, until out came, "YEESSSS." After several more questions got one-word answers, I was wondering what good was a telling tool for a kid who couldn't talk.

I was searching for a polite excuse to bow out gracefully when his speech teacher took over. She reminded Jake he already had a family story he could storyboard, one he'd gotten for the eighth-grade family tree project. When I came back to the trailer the next day at break, I saw his first storyboard. The speech teacher had made him a board with big yellow sticky notes. I scanned the sheet, and I was not encouraged. His stick figure pictures were very basic, loose scrawls that were hard to read, and he had only a few key words on the whole sheet.

I swallowed hard, but the speech teacher beamed at me, and suggested that Jake tell me his story. Jake nodded and pointed to the first square. It looked like a stick figure in the middle with four tiny figures sort of floating on each side. I thought of angels. Jake pointed at the middle figure and said in his slow slurred speech something like, "Myyy gaaaat-gannnnnfaaaather, cudd hoooool up foooour women at ooooonccccce." I was lost. The speech teacher smiled at me as if this was great. I hung on. Jake pointed to square 2: a stick figure and something that might be a stick animal? Jake slurred, "Heeee cuuudddd puuuut hisss hed in a liiioooons mouuuuth."

Desperate and reaching for some handle, I pointed to the animal-like scrawl and asked, "Is that a lion?" Jake nodded and the speech teacher

beamed at me. Then the lights went on. I said, "Is his head in the lion's mouth?" Jake nodded. I asked, "Is he in the circus?" Jake nodded again, but now he was frowning at me like I must be stupid, and the speech teacher was laughing.

She said, "His great-grandfather was a circus performer in Poland. Apparently he was famous, a strong man; see how he's holding four women up, and there's more."

Holy cow! Jake had essentially made a visual list of things his great-grandfather did. But what a list: lifting four women on his outstretched arms, taming the lion, being shot from a cannon, lying down for a truck to drive over him, holding back a steam engine. And Jake had thrown in some family history, too. His great-grandfather, the strongman, had 17 children, so his great-grandmother was pretty strong, too!

Jake's story ended with a stick man lying down, "He died in his sleep at 102 years old. In his own bed." I sat back and looked at Jake. He smiled at me like he had been waiting for me to catch up.

I tried. The break was over, so talking fast, I told Jake his storyboard was a great beginning, but I showed him how his pictures and key words could communicate more. Rather than drawing just the cannon, he could show a figure flying out of the cannon, and write "BOOM" in big letters.

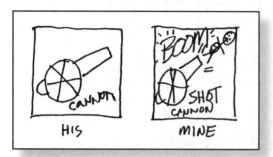

And I suggested he could add a simple introduction, an opening square that might say something like, "My great-grandfather could do amazing things. He was a star. . . ." As I left, he still had that laser-focus look, and I still wasn't sure how much he understood, but I hoped his speech teacher would help him.

When I came back a couple of weeks later to hear the Language Arts students share their stories, I went out during the break to see if Jake was in the trailer. The speech teacher was excited as she showed me his finished book. He had typed his text and pasted his drawings in below. His illustrations were still basic stick pictures, but bigger and a lot clearer. His teacher said, "Jake wants to read this to you."

Jake sat next to me, opened his book carefully, looked at me, and started to read, "My great-grandfather was in the circus. . . ." I was amazed how he read; the words came out a little slower than common speech, but they were distinct and pleasing. He was pointing to his typed words, telling his story with confidence, using his book as a practiced speaking script. I guessed the pictures helped him to know his audience was with him, but his voice was clear. When he finished, we laughed at his great-grandfather's story. I was so glad Jake had stuck with me.

Jake Teaches

After Jake left, his speech teacher and I discussed how powerful storyboards were for Jake as a speech and writing tool. She said, "We could tell

Jake liked storyboarding, and then we discovered him using the drawing for other things. We found him 'taking it to the next level,'" she smiled. "He was taking a social studies test in class, drawing little pictures next to test questions. We figured out he was brainstorming his ideas in pictures before he tried to write text."

Jake had made the leap adults can easily miss. He figured out that drawing was not just a writing tool—it was a

brainstorming and thinking tool, a fast way to get ideas out of his head and onto paper. Jake was brainstorming in pictures, something we all do unconsciously, and then putting his mental pictures on paper to help focus his text.

I've now seen many teachers use the power of storyboards as a note-taking, test preparation, content reinforcement tool. But it needs to be said that it was students like Jake who taught their teachers about visual tools. Often the students who find adult text tools don't work well for them make this leap first. Once again, this is the essence of differentiated learning—students like Jake showing us that they are visual learners *just like us*, only they are just a little faster at it than we are.

LOCKED LEARNING

If we are serious about mainstreaming students with disabilities, we need to give them the visual tools that will help them and help their classmates engage with them. Storyboards for reading and writing create a learning circle that invites everyone in. The opposite can be true. A text-only focus in the classroom creates a split that separates learners and disables everybody.

I was working with a group of first graders in the library. They were storyboarding *The Three Little Pigs*. We had a good time drawing fat pigs and coming up with a scary wolf. Someone had a breakthrough, discovering through the storyboard that the story is clearly a repeat of the same sequence three times: building houses and that wolf going through his huffing and puffing routine. We discussed that repeat pattern and how it builds and reinforces the logic of the story. A storyboard helps everyone see and discuss the big picture.

While we worked, I noticed a boy in the back of the room, maybe a sixth grader, at a table with an adult. It wasn't hard to guess he was Special Ed. He was hunched over doing some paperwork, but he kept looking at us, and eventually he just watched what the kids were doing.

When the first graders left, he walked up and said, "I was watching you." He looked at me with real intensity. I told him we were storyboarding *The Three Little Pigs*.

He said, "I know. I could do that."

I handed him the marker, told him to start with the first pig going out into the world—whom does he meet? The boy drew two spider-like shapes in the first square. In the next box, he put a rectangle. There were no key words. I stopped him, worried. I asked him to tell me what he had so far. He pointed to the spiders in first box and said, "This is the pig, and this is the man with straw." They looked identical. He pointed to the rectangle and said, "This is the house."

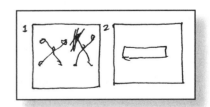

I was stuck: these pictures weren't communicating much, and his telling was bare-bones. His pictures didn't free him to tell; instead, they actually stopped the telling, because he had to explain his symbols. Still, I had the feeling I'd seen those spider figures before. Then I remembered another eighth-grade student I'd worked with, one who was labeled autistic. He had made figures a lot like this. These were the personal symbols a preschooler might make, useful to young children until they realized their pictures weren't communicating meaning, couldn't be recognized by others.

By first grade, most kids are aware that drawing is about you and your audience. They learn how to make an identifiable stick person. They know that a stick figure is powerful shorthand that communicates easily that this is a human being. I looked at this boy and wondered why he was so stuck. He seemed mentally locked. Couldn't he see these scrawls don't communicate? What in his brain made him insist on making rigid private symbols that were unrecognizable?

I was ready to quit. It was clear to me storyboarding wasn't going to work for him. But I was curious. It was my break, and he had initiated this, so I decided to do a small experiment to see what he did know about symbol

making. I said, "That's not the way I draw a pig. A pig is fat, so I make him round like this."

I drew a circle body, then a smaller circle head and a circle nose, while talking about a pig's round nose. (If I had access to a picture of a real pig, that would have been better.) When my pig was done, we talked about how well it communicated. He agreed it looked a little like a snowman. I asked him what else I could add to my picture to make sure other people knew this was a pig. He suggested, "A curly tail."

I wanted to shout "Okay!" For the first time I knew he was aware of shared symbols, tuned in to some basics of picture communication; he knew the common symbol for a pig's tail. Maybe he could do more. I pointed to his next picture. I said, "It's hard for me to know that's a house. The way

most kids draw a house is with a pointed roof. I drew, keeping it icon-simple. He nodded seriously, said "Oh, okay," like I just told him something useful, a good thing to know. Then I showed him a basic stick figure of a man: arms, legs, head, trunk. He watched with focus, nodded, and smiled like that made sense too. I hoped it did.

I asked him to try storyboarding the pig's story again. He went at it, and I could see it was going pretty well, his pictures now basic but recognizable, round pigs, stick people, until he got to the wolf. "I don't know how to make

a wolf." I told him lots of kids and teachers don't. We worked on making a wolf, discussing symbolmaking and communication. We decided a wolf needed a long nose and big teeth. In a few minutes, he had done a passable storyboard of the basic story, one anyone who knew the children's classic might recognize. I said, "Pretty good." He beamed at me.

I was pleased to see how easily he was able to let go of his programmed, rigid drawings, and to see how eagerly he picked up on a basic picture code that could communicate. At the same time, I found myself angry and sad that no one had bothered to teach him some basic drawing skills he could use to really communicate.

I spoke to his teacher, who had watched us from afar, apparently amused by this diversion from the usual drill. She confirmed he had autism and few text skills. In a few sentences, it was clear he was getting lots of text drills but little exposure to drawing as a way to show what he knows. I suggested they might give him some basic drawing lessons. She seemed interested but she said she was "only an aide," not in a position to change his program. Then she explained, "Drawing is not in his Individualized Education Program."

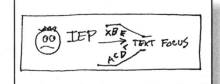

It's not hard to guess that what was in his "individualized" program was the same basic individual program used everywhere: First and foremost, he must learn using text skills. His school had spent thousands of hours teaching this boy to draw the 26 basic symbol pictures we value in school. Abstract forms like A, B, C, and of course, X, the symbol for "cross something out," which was ironically the same symbol he used for person or pig. It only took that boy one look at storyboarding to come forward and say, "I can do that." Then he patiently taught me, and his aide, how to teach him.

He was *so ready* to communicate with us, so ready to be taught to make meaningful symbols. Once he got used to sequencing ideas in pictures, sharing content visually and verbally, then he could begin to add more abstract symbols, learn to integrate those text symbols with pictures to communicate more.

Labels, like pictures, are powerful tools. They can help us find common ground with others or they can help keep us apart. I wonder what label this boy might apply to adults so locked on a narrow set of text skills that they prefer he draw rigid abstract letterforms over and over and over, even when they don't help him communicate much.

It's easy to imagine a different literacy landscape, one with fewer "different learners" and fewer "learning disabilities." It's not hard to imagine kids (and adults) using drawing and telling to become more comfortable engaged writers, more versatile thinkers, better communicators. Certainly, students who use storyboards and telling fluently will be better public

speakers, better able to handle spontaneous collaboration, better able to think on their feet, better prepared to design the tools of the visual future and to do the kind of shared writing and multimedia teaching we need. Perhaps most important, students taught to value a broader definition of literacy would know that all students (even the kid alone in the library) are ready to be included and share what they know.

I'd already written the paragraph above, about imagining a change in learners with different tools, when I got a call from a teacher who'd been using storyboards with her second graders for a number of years. She was telling me how visual verbal tools had become a central feature of her classroom community, and were especially helpful for kids who were struggling with literacy. Then she told me she had recently gone to a school talent show. She said, "As I watched kids get up to perform I was struck by how many of the students on stage were the very kids who'd come to my room struggling, hesitant, withdrawn. Those kids thrived with drawing and telling. It was those same kids who now had a natural confidence with an audience. They were spontaneous and engaged, with a lot to share." She didn't have to imagine how kids might grow with visual/verbal tools that pull everyone into the literacy circle.

Appendix A

Introduction to a Visual Story-Building Workshop

Below is an attempt to re-create the way I introduce storyboards as a story-building tool to an audience of students. Feel free to use this information as a guide, adapting the material as you see fit for your students. For this introduction to storyboarding, you will need a large class storyboard, one that can easily be revised—for example, squares drawn on a whiteboard. This presentation builds on basic picture-writing skills we've already discussed. Please bear with me if I've repeated some of this information because it builds in a logical sequence kids find easy to follow.

A CLASSROOM INTRO TO PICTURE WRITING

I first introduce the storyboard process by retelling a well-known story, be it *The Three Little Pigs* for grade 3 and younger, or some other familiar tale for older kids. During this retelling, I introduce the basic elements of storyboards—the stick pictures and the key words—as I provide an overview of the story-building process.

I begin by showing students how picture-writing works. "I'm going to tell a big story. You'll see what a good storyteller I am. I'm going to draw in this first square. Just shout it out when you think you know what story I'm telling."

These are the first two squares of my storyboard. Despite the simple pics, most folks recognize the story before I get my second square done.

"Yes, this is the story of the Titanic. Let me tell you the story. You'll see I'm a great storyteller, very efficient. Here's my telling in two squares:

1. The biggest ship in the world, the Titanic (pointing to the second square)
2. Sunk. THE END. Pretty good, huh?"

When kids protest that I left a lot out, I tell them they're right—no one can tell a big story well in two squares. I ask students what's missing from my story. When someone mentions the iceberg, I agree that I left out this important "hook."

DEVELOPING THE HOOK

To tell a story well, it's important to have some kind of hook. The hook is the most interesting part of a story; it's what draws people in.

Storyboards can make basic story-building easier for many kids, but it is essential to understand we are using the same basic steps of the writing process. Storyboards make it easier to get to the heart of good storytelling. I'm showing here that the best place to start is not at the beginning but with the hook—the main idea.

I redraw my storyboard in three squares, adding the iceberg. I intentionally re-draw the ship as a lump.

Before I get a chance to add to my story, someone will comment that my ship looks like a birthday cake and that my iceberg looks like a triangle. I agree with that and wonder aloud how people who can't draw very well can work with storyboards. I suggest we make a rule that drawing well doesn't matter. We agree as a class that if students can't tell what a picture is, they won't say, "Your drawing stinks," because drawing doesn't matter. But it's okay to say, "I'm not sure what that is." Then the person making that comment can work with you to help you fix the picture.

Once everyone agrees to that rule, I go to the next level. I ask, "How can we be sure everyone will know this is the Titanic?" In younger grades this provides an interesting peek into gender and literacy politics. Boys will often tell me how I can improve my drawing, "Add port holes and..." Girls will usually be the first to suggest I could just write the word *Titanic*.

I write TITNC in big letters over the picture. There is a lot of squirming before someone says "You spelled it wrong." That leads to the second and

more controversial rule: For the purposes of our storyboarding, especially at the beginning of the process, *spelling doesn't matter*. (See also page 95, Spelling Note.)

Once we've got the rules about drawing and spelling out of the way, we can get on with storytelling. I note for kids that in each square of my storyboard I include both a picture and a key word. I ask for both, because that way the "picture-smart folks" and the "text-smart folks" can all read my story.

I add "Titnc" and "Ice" and then I do a review: "From now on, if you see a big triangle in this story, what is it?"

We agree that it's an iceberg. We are creating a "code" for my story. Someone said I should tell everybody the Titanic set sail from England so you'll notice I've put an E in the corner of the ship square; that's to remind me. Often just a letter will remind a teller what to say.

Here's my new second-draft telling, with the hook added to my story:

1. The biggest ship in the world, the Titanic, set sail from England.

2. In the middle of the ocean it hit a big iceberg.

3. It sank. The end.

I suggest to the students that my story is complete. It has the main events: a beginning, a middle, and an end, and it also has a good hook. Of course, there is protest that I still left a lot out. I ask, "What's missing?" Very often I'll get this answer immediately: "You need more details!" It's an interesting answer, one that goes to the heart of storytelling and writing. Let me show you why "details" are not what we want, in fact, why "details" is a word that can confuse kids.

My response is to show this picture. I say the dots are to remind me to tell the details.

Let's tell this as a three-square story now. Let me tell that first square again with details: "The Titanic, the biggest ship in the world, set sail from England and had 3,777 rivets in its hull. Each of those rivets creaked and groaned. Those rivets weighed three and a half ounces each, and they were made in a small factory in Shropshire where the workers all ate silver sardines for lunch...."

In one classroom a boy interrupted, "That's a *riveting* story." I laughed and said, "This is riveting, but is that what you want to know about the Titanic? Who knows how many shoelaces there were on the Titanic? Is that a great detail, too?"

I explain that details are exactly what we don't want at this stage of storytelling. "Details" is a word that works for adults, but it diverts young storytellers from the task at hand. We don't want details—not yet—not until the main events in our story are in place. Details will come when we're almost done. Then details will add resonance and authenticity.

Here we want to know the "good stuff." I know that doesn't sound very specific, but if I ask kids to list some of the good stuff in the story of the Titanic, they get this idea right away. They will tell me, "When the man jumps off the ship and hits the propeller . . . ." They quickly figure out that the "good stuff" in some stories is really the "bad stuff"!

If I ask, "What's more bad stuff in the story?" I will get lots more. Here are three examples:

- ■ One lifeboat crashing onto another
- ■ People trapped below deck
- ■ Ship flooding

BUILDING A STORYBOARD AROUND A HOOK

A first draft diagram of the Titanic story: beginning, middle, and end

The teller's job is to know how to tell the important stuff related to the hook. If the story is sad, then we want to hear the sad stuff. If the story is funny, we want the funny stuff. If a story is scary, we want the scary stuff, and so on.

Storytelling is communicating with your audience. The idea here is that knowing the hook, the main thrust of your story, and finding what's worth telling around the hook, is the teller's job. Next, I show kids how their story will be built around the hook.

I point to the board and say, "It's hard to tell a good story in three squares, especially a story with a good hook. Let's see if we can tell the story of the Titanic using this entire storyboard." My white board has 13 squares like a small storyboard sheet. I draw the ship in the upper left. I put the iceberg square somewhere in the middle of the board, and in the bottom square I write, "Sunk."

We are looking at the beginning, the middle, and the end of the story, but I don't say that. Those are terms that have little meaning for many kids. But here that abstract idea is a visible reality. I tell them all stories are built around the hook. This story starts in England, builds up to the iceberg crash, and then it unfolds from the crash. Of course the tragic story of the Titanic has lots of "bad stuff," a cascading series of smaller hooks after the crash.

At left is my first try at storyboarding the Titanic, putting the whole story in 13 squares. For many students, this storyboard will be the first time they see what beginning, middle, and end mean. They can see that there are four empty squares available until we get to the iceberg, and six squares until the ship sinks.

BUILD UP AND DOWN FROM THE HOOK

Our main job in storyboarding is to figure out how to build up to the hook and then tell what happens after. Students will realize that all the bad stuff in the Titanic happens *after the ship hits the iceberg*. They will realize we need to move the iceberg forward in the story if we want to have enough squares to show all the bad stuff. Generally, kids can come up with two or three essential squares before the iceberg, and many squares after for their telling. I usually suggest we add two squares at the bottom of the page and then move the iceberg up. Here's my basic storyboard of the Titanic.

Revised diagram allows more room for story development

You'll see I've drawn story content in three squares (2, 4, and 15) to show how I might tell the story. My first new square (2) is a picture of the captain. He had a beard, and you can see he's wearing a little cap. From now on when someone has a cap like that, you know that's a crew member. I show him saying "Full Steam . . ." but I tell the rest: "'. . . ahead, we're the biggest ship in the world, we can't be sunk.' Foreshadowing, wiggling the hook that's coming at your audience."

In the square just before the iceberg, I draw another face wearing a cap. Who is he, and what is he saying? Kids can usually guess that he's

the lookout. Fourth graders will tell you he's saying something like, "Oh, no!" If I'm working with high school students, someone will suggest he is saying something more pungent.

When I write "Oh, no!" next to the face and ask the class to read back to me what it

says, the kids read, "Oh, no" quietly. Then I write it big, and when I ask the students to read that back to me, they shout, "OH, NO!" which is what I want. I then ask students to brainstorm what they might put in the empty squares of the storyboard. I suggest everyone try this on his or her own. Then I have students share their pictures and discuss what they've decided to put in and what to leave out.

If students ask if they can use more squares to tell the story, I suggest they try to stay with this one sheet. Telling a big story in a limited space on a storyboard is a great real-world exercise. The average children's picture book has 14 spreads (a spread is two facing pages).

EXPANDING THE HOOK

A metaphor I use for story building with the storyboard is expanding the hook. Every story is built around the hook. This helps kid to know what to put in and what to leave out, and it emphasizes the idea that the story is supposed to communicate. The hook is the reason people want to hear your story, so the more your story stays with the hook, the better.

The Titanic is an ideal story to use to introduce the idea of expanding the hook, because this is a straightforward accident story, and all accident stories work the same way: We build up to the crash and then we show what resulted from the crash.

If the story is about a girl crashing her bike, the first time she tells it, the hook will often go like this, in three squares: I saw the tree. I hit the tree. I got hurt. Any hook worth telling deserves more than three squares. Here's a retelling of this hook: I saw the tree. I tried to put on my brakes. "Who wants to see a close-up of the tires skidding?" I realized I was going to hit the tree. "Who wants a close-up of her face as she's about to hit that tree?" Then there's a good crash square. Was there blood after the crash? "Who wants to see a close-up of the bleeding?" By the time we're done, we will have expanded the hook to take six or seven squares. Then we will see if there are stitches. That will be a second hook, going to get stitches. Everybody wants to know more about that, too.

A three-square telling of any good hook is easily expanded to allow telling all the good stuff (significant details).

Of course this idea of expanding the hook can be applied to any story, and help both the teller and the audience to focus on the good stuff, the sad or silly or funny part of the hook. As you use storyboards, you'll see close-ups are essential to expanding the range of emotions in kids' stories.

It's impossible to write, "She was worried" with this picture. That's why storyboards bring better writing. When we tell from exciting pictures, we tend to write exciting sentences, too.

GOING ON A STORY HUNT

I often introduce storyboarding as a creative writing tool by having kids collect a family story to work with. I find family stories are the easiest way to get everybody going.

It is essential that to storyboard, or write, students have to have something to say before they begin. To ask students to storyboard or to write about nothing is a waste of time; however, to just say, "Come up with a topic" will lead to predictable failure for those less comfortable with text. When I work with a new group of students I want them to have something that is theirs to write about, getting family stories through a Story Hunt is ideal. Family stories are a great way for me to get to know kids quickly. Often their stories give me big clues to who they are, how their families see themselves, and how I can best engage them.

Each student will build his or her own story, but I suggest the class start story building with everyone working together on a common story before going it alone. It is easy to try Shared Writing as an all-class process using a well-known story. I prefer starting a class on story-building with nonfiction ✶ writing. Family stories are ideal, because we can refer to real events to discuss characters and action. Indeed, retelling a family story gives kids a big leg up because the basic story already exists in a first draft; they will refine the draft they have heard.

At the same time, my hope is that by the time we're done working on a student's story, students will be able to tell the story better than they heard it. Certainly they will create a new telling of the story for their family. When we begin to revise their stories, it is easier with nonfiction to discuss what fits and what doesn't. We all know Martians did not land at Uncle Fred's birthday party, even if the story seems to need some added excitement. We can discuss what is worth telling when we have real characters and events to work with.

As we saw in the opening of Chapter 8, sharing and writing stories in the classroom is a great way to build community. A back-to-school night where kids get up and read their family stories can be a real event. A girl's story about Mom saving her little brother when he fell through the ice can get the whole cafeteria focused. But to get good stories we need to help kids connect with a workable story.

The first time I tried a family Story Hunt, I got only a 60 percent return rate. Many kids said they didn't get a story, or their family didn't have stories. Of course all families have stories, but they may not share them regularly, or parents may not be very good storytellers themselves. I found it helped everyone to send home a Story Hunt sheet to prime the story pump. With this sheet, the return rate on stories jumps dramatically, and the stories kids get are more dramatic and easier to use for writing.

Teachers should adapt the sheet to fit their grade level and needs. The key here is to ask for stories with a hook. One school asked for town history, another for old stories about the school itself, another for immigrant stories, and another for accident stories.

SAMPLE STORY HUNT SHEET

Dear Families,

Our class is "hunting" and "collecting" stories. These stories may be old (about Grandma sleepwalking long ago) or new (Tommy got a bean stuck in his ear). Try to help your child find a story with a good HOOK, something funny, scary, stupid, sad or dramatic about a story. The hook is the reason kids want to hear that story.

Here are some places to hunt for stories. Please add your own!

Tell your kids a story about:

- The dumbest/most foolish/most embarrassing thing you did as a kid (could be a story about grandparents, aunts, uncles, neighbors)
- Accidents, broken bones, stitches
- Storms, floods, fires
- A time when you were in trouble, lost
- A time when you were really scared
- Family nonsense, strange relatives, unusual events
- Christmas, Hanukkah, other holidays or traditions
- Strange family pets or wild animals

Here's a story we've heard today—with a real hook!

My mother lived in Holden, Massachusetts, when she was growing up. City cousins came to visit. City cousins were scared of everything—especially wild animals—and got teased about it constantly. City cousin Jean was afraid to swim, but we teased and she dove in. She came up screaming with a snapping turtle on her arm. We didn't tease her anymore.

Thanks for helping your child hunt down these treasures!

As in the sample above, I generally include a short example story at the bottom of the sheet. This sample story is most useful if it comes from a student or a teacher, and it's best if every student has heard the full story told. The written version on the sheet is condensed to a bare-bones telling of the story kids heard. I then encourage kids to share the full story with their family.

No Text to Start

One big reason storyboards help get everybody going is that they let students try out writing ideas before they commit to "real" writing. In fact, text can often slow down the story-building process. Students can show you it is important to hold off on text at the start of the process.

Let me give an example. Third graders were sharing hooks of their family stories. Several students had shared stories about a famous flood, when the local river had gone over its banks and flooded the neighborhood for blocks around the school. Finally, everyone had offered hooks except for two kids. I asked a girl if she had a story. She looked tentative; I glanced at the teacher, who said she had a story. I asked what her hook was. The girl hesitated again, looking to the teacher. The teacher told her to look at her paper. Then the girl unfolded a page of text. Her mom had written the story out to help the girl remember it. It was all there in text, but the girl couldn't summarize it. She had to read the story from the beginning.

I suggested in an aside to the teacher that this was an example of the way text can block a story. I wasn't sure the teacher believed me until a boy two rows back said he didn't know if his story had a hook. I asked him to tell the story so we could see. When he produced a text summary of the story he'd heard, the teacher looked at me like I'd paid these two kids off to make a point: Text can block text.

After class the teacher was dumbfounded, telling me the girl who had struggled was generally one of her best students. The boy, Rodrigo, was not a writer, but he always had a story to tell. Both kids had been given text by adults to help them, and both kids had trouble sharing their story.

This is a revealing twist in a text-focused classroom. We've found that students who bring a text version of their family story from home, one they've written themselves or one a parent has provided "to remind them of the details," often have trouble summarizing and sharing their stories. If kids get a story with a good hook, they can usually retell the story. Having a text sheet to consult slows them down, and often locks them up. They get locked into the particular wording on the page and they can't spontaneously share or expand on the story. What's more, going to text before sharing can make revision much more difficult.

Appendix B

Board Formats

Here are three basic storyboard formats designed to support learners for many literacy tasks. As we've seen, these formats can stand alone or be used in combinations that create a logical path from brainstorming to content organization to creating well-organized text.

Page 136

Storyboards with a set of basic squares are an all-purpose brainstorming, sequencing, writing tool.

Page 137

Storyboards with lines below the squares support note taking and content review. This format helps students highlight key information with images.

Page 138

This format helps students make a clear transition from image to text, allowing the writer to see his or her final work in a traditional text block.

Teachers can create many custom formats that make targeted tasks easier for students. The compare/contrast format below at left lends itself to both content reinforcement and to organizing ideas for a persuasive essay. The storyboard handout shown below at right offers visuals and text laid out in a sequence to engage learners and guide them through a multi-step task.

Page 139

Page 140

This format, with opposing squares and writing lines between, allows students to place images and ideas across from each other. It works well for compare-and-contrast tasks and persuasive essay development (pros on one side and cons on the other). Lines in between can reinforce connections or highlight differences.

This handout serves as my visual script and students' sequencing notes for the process of creating a story and setting it in a picture-book format. For notes on how I integrate it into my teaching, see Chapter 7.

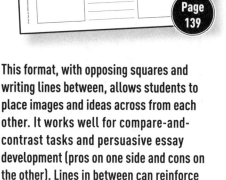

These formats are easily generated using the "drawing tools" on any standard word-processing program and can be adjusted to fit the needs of any classroom. The basic rule of thumb in creating user-friendly storyboards is larger squares for younger students. Older students can handle more tightly packed squares and more information within each square.

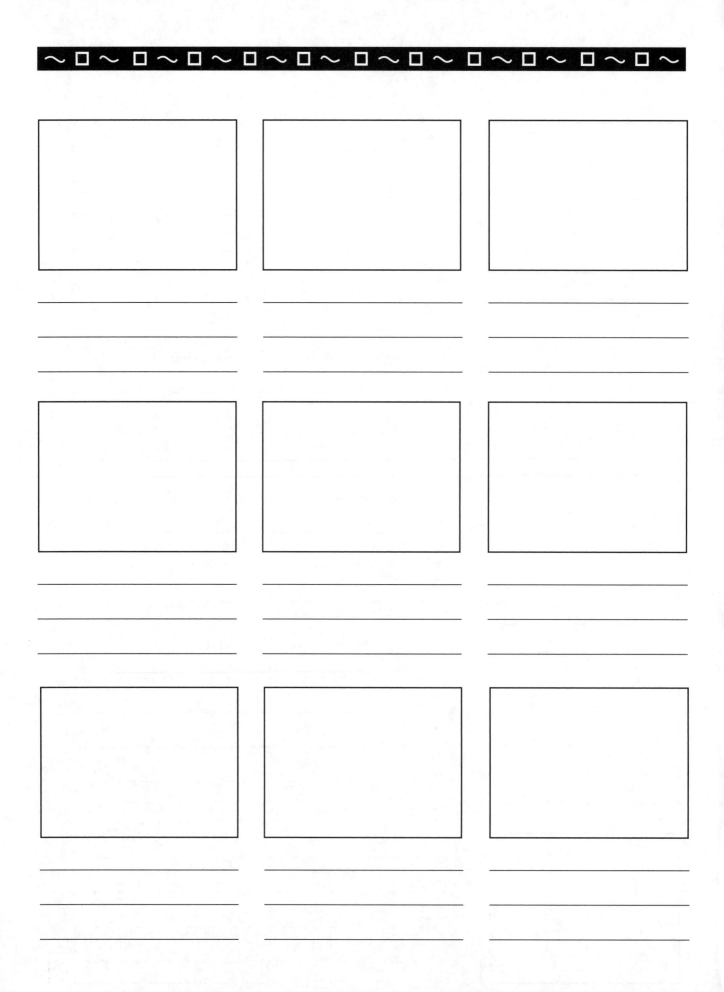

Steps for Creating a Story and Picture Book

References

Armstrong, T. (2000). *In their own way: Discovering and encouraging your child's multiple intelligences* (rev. ed.). New York: Tarcher.

Atwell, N. (1987). *In the middle: Writing, reading, and learning with adolescents.* Portsmouth, NH: Boynton-Cook.

Beers, K., Probst, R., & Rief, L., Eds. (2007). *Adolescent literacy: Turning promise into practice.* Portsmouth, NH: Heinemann.

Bell, N. (1986). *Visualizing and verbalizing for language comprehension and thinking.* Paso Robles, CA: Academy of Reading Publications.

Bell, N. (1991). Gestalt imagery: A critical factor in language comprehension. *Annals of Dyslexia*, 41. Retrieved October 16, 2007, from http://www.lindamoodbell.com/downloads/pdf/research/Gestalt.pdf

Fueyo, J. A. (1991). Language arts classrooms: Spaces where anything can happen. *Writing Teacher* (Sept).

Graves, D. H. (1984). *A researcher learns to write.* Exeter, NH: Heinemann.

Graves, D. H. (1989). *Investigate nonfiction.* Portsmouth, NH: Heinemann.

Hess, M. A. (1999). Although some voice doubts, advocates say differentiated instruction can raise the bar for all learners. Retrieved October 16, 2007, from http://weac.org/kids/1998-99/march99/differ.htm

Keene, E. O. & Zimmermann, S. (1997). *Mosaic of thought: Teaching comprehension in a reader's workshop.* Portsmouth, NH: Heinemann.

Levine, M. (2003). *The myth of laziness.* New York: Simon & Schuster.

Rozin, P., Porisky, S., & Sotsky, R. (1971). American children with reading problems can easily learn to read English represented by Chinese characters. *Science* 171, 1264-1267.

Smith, M. W. & Wilhelm, J. D. (2000). *Reading don't fix no Chevys: Literacy in the lives of young men.* Portsmouth, NH: Heinemann.

Strasser, T. (1981). *The wave.* New York: Dell.

Index